Battlegrou

Saint-Nazaire

With the continued expansion of the Battleground Series a **Battleground Series Club** has been formed to benefit the reader. The purpose of the Club is to keep members informed of new titles and to offer many other reader-benefits. Membership is free and by registering an interest you can help us predict print runs and thus assist us in maintaining the quality and prices at their present levels.

Please call the office on 01226 734555, or send your name and address along with a request for more information to:

Battleground Series Club Pen & Sword Books Ltd,
47 Church Street, Barnsley, South Yorkshire S70 2AS

Battleground Europe

Saint-Nazaire

James Dorrian

Pen & Sword
MILITARY

This book is dedicated to all those Nazairiens who fought and suffered in the cause of freedom

First published in Great Britain in 2006 by
Pen & Sword Military
an imprint of
Pen & Sword Books Ltd
47 Church Street
Barnsley
South Yorkshire
S70 2AS

ISBN 1844153347

A CIP catalogue record for this book is
available from the British Library

Typeset in Palatino

Printed and bound in the United Kingdom by CPI

Pen & Sword Books Ltd incorporates the Imprints of Pen & Sword Aviation,Pen
& Sword Maritime, Pen & Sword Military, Wharncliffe Local History, Pen and
Sword Select, Pen and Sword Military Classics and Leo Cooper.
For a complete list of Pen & Sword titles, please contact
Pen & Sword Books Limited
47 Church Street, Barnsley, South Yorkshire, S70 2AS, England
E-mail: enquiries@pen-and-sword.co.uk
Website: www.pen-and-sword.co.uk

CONTENTS

The survivors of the battle between ML*306* and *Jaguar* are brought ashore Saturday morning. Stoker Butcher is assisted by Ordinary Seaman Batteson, left of picture, and Lieutenant Ronnie Swayne.

FOREWORD

I am very honoured to write the foreword to Jim Dorrian's excellent guide to the scene of operations of the Saint-Nazaire raid. Jim cleary and vividly describes the events of the operation, his account further brought to life by eye-witness accounts.

We in the Commandos were all volunteers. We did not live in barracks but were paid an allowance and lived in billets, mainly in seaside towns near where we trained and where we were made tremendously welcome. We were expected to think for ourselves, and our training resulted in our being outstandingly fit and tough – excellent at shooting and in battlefield skills. There was only one punishment in the Commandos – no Confined to Barracks, no detention, only the dreaded RTU Returned to Unit.

MAJOR GENERAL CORRAN PURDON, CBE, MC, CPM, Légion d' Honneur
CORRAN PURDON

Some of us who took part in Operation CHARIOT had been in action already – France 1940, the Norwegian campaign, raids on the Channel Islands and the French coast, the First and Second Lofoten Islands and the Vaagso raid. We all thirsted for action, we were young, cheerful, confident, convinced that we were a Corps d'Elite – we were a band of brothers.

Representatives of all the Army Commandos stationed in the United Kingdom took part in the raid, with No 2 Commando providing the assault and protection parties, and the remaining units – Nos 1, 3, 4, 5, 6, 9 and 12 Commandos – supplying the demolition teams: we were all in on the act. As Jim points out, the dock demolitions were all successfully completed within thirty minutes, and when the five tons of high explosive in the bows of HMS *Campbeltown* detonated at 1130 hrs destroying the southern dock gate, the entire dry dock was put out of action for the remainder of the war. Micky Wynn's two delayed-action torpedoes fired from MTB *74* against the outer pair of lock gates in the Old Entrance completed the destruction.

The aim of the operation, to deny repair facilities in the giant 'Normandie' dock to the *Tirpitz* (and to any other German battleship) was successfully accomplished. As you go around the scene of action, following the route recommended by Jim Dorrian in this comprehensive guide, think of the young, eager sailors and Commandos in the days when England was England. We believed it was worth dying for. Morale was sky high; most of us had made dates with our wives, fiancées or girl-friends for the next weekend. When we realised there were no ships to take us home, Jim's guide describes how we who survived fought our way into the town, intending to reach home by way of Spain.

Those of us who got back to England or were captured felt, and feel yet, a bond of brotherhood personified in the Saint-Nazaire Society. We are very proud that five of our members were awarded the Victoria Cross for their actions during the raid, these including the VCs awarded to two superbly brave fighting men – Able Seaman Bill Savage of MGB *314*, and Sergeant Tom Durrant of No 1 Commando (the only Army VC awarded in a naval action).

Perhaps as you stand in the British Military cemetery at Escoublac, or in front of our memorial in the Place Verdun in Saint-Nazaire, you will think, as I always do, of our fallen comrades-in-arms, and of the words of the Kohima epitaph,

> When you go home, tell them of us and say,
> for your tomorrow, we gave our today.

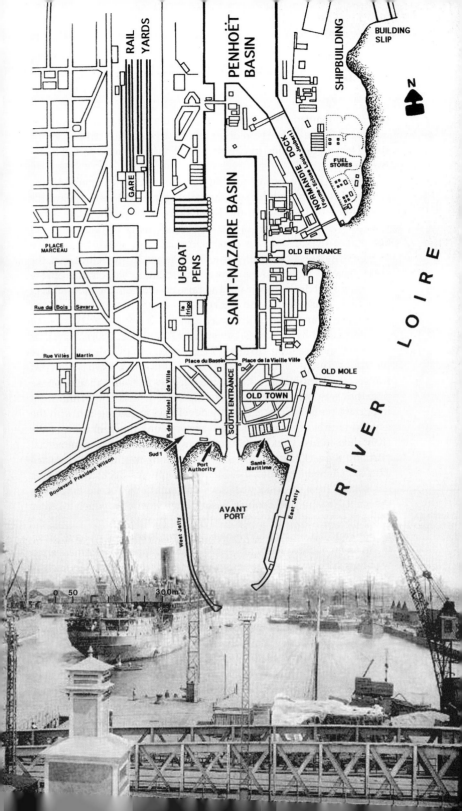

RAIL YARDS

PENHOËT BASIN

SHIPBUILDING

BUILDING SLIP

N

GARE

NORMANDIE DOCK
(Forme-Écluse Louis Joubert)

FUEL STORES

PLACE MARCEAU

SAINT-NAZAIRE BASIN

U-BOAT PENS

OLD ENTRANCE

Rue du Bois Savary

le frigo

Rue Villès Martin

Place du Bassin

Place de la Vieille Ville

OLD MOLE

R. de l'Hotel de Ville

OLD TOWN

SOUTH ENTRANCE

Sud 1

Port Authority

Santé Maritime

RIVER LOIRE

Boulevard Président Wilson

West Jetty

AVANT PORT

East Jetty

0   50   300m

INTRODUCTION

On 25 September, 2003, at high tide on the evening of a sparkling autumn day, the 150,000 ton ocean liner *Queen Mary 2* slipped gently from Dock C, her fitting out berth in the French Atlantic port of Saint-Nazaire.

Under her own power for the very first time, shepherded by a flotilla of tugs and pilot boats, the great ship eased slowly seawards along the broad estuary of the River Loire to begin the trials which would shortly culminate in the raising of the red ensign and her acceptance by Cunard. Towering some 200 feet above the sea, the aseptic whiteness of her superstructure warmed by the setting sun, the sheer majesty of her presence was sufficient to stop traffic on the sweeping Pont de Saint-Nazaire and raise cheers from the thousands of expectant 'Nazairiens' who packed the quays, the jetties and the shoreline east and south of the town.

Constructed by Alstom-Chantiers de l'Atlantique, *Queen Mary 2* is the latest and grandest creation of the various shipyards which, over the course of the eighteenth and nineteenth centuries, have helped transform Saint-Nazaire from the sleepy fishing village whose potential was first recognized by Napoleon 1, into one of the most important ports in France. Initially developed in conjunction with the Clydeside firm of John Scott, these sweep along the right bank of the river, their industry and bustle conjoining with that of the commercial port and the facilities of Airbus. Encompassing much of the eastward extension of Saint-Nazaire, the Chantiers' slipways, docks and gantries are isolated from the residential developments of the Second Empire by the Saint-Nazaire and Penhoët Basins, huge wet docks which together extend for almost a mile to the north of the Avant Port.

For almost a century and a half these yards and basins have given life to an enviable dynasty of vessels, both military and commercial; to warships such as *Strasbourg* and *Jean-Bart*, and to opulent liners such as *Paris*, *Ile de France* and the beautiful, inimitable *Normandie*, the scale and grandeur of whose construction during the years immediately preceding the Second World War would serve to redefine not only the engineering potential of the port, but also its physical form.

At 80,000 tons very much the giant of her day, *Normandie* entered service in 1935 her speed and luxury speaking volumes for the particular skills of the Penhoët yard, the organization contracted to build her for the 'French Line'. Designed for the singular purpose of pampering the rich and famous as they travelled in style between Europe and America, there was a certain irony in the fact that her own

The liner *Normandie* passing through the dry dock on her way to the Loire estuary. ECOMUSEE DE SAINT-NAZAIRE-FONDS BOURGUEIL (EDOUARD)

journey to completion during the depression years had been characterized above all else by acute shortages of cash: for in addition to the financial strain imposed by her groundbreaking construction, the extent to which *Normandie* would dwarf existing facilities required major, and expensive, alterations to the structure of the port itself, giving Saint-Nazaire the configuration that would become familiar to planners of both sides during the war years. Prior to her keel being laid it was necessary to construct a completely new building slip, in addition to which excavations began at an early stage for the vast new lock by means of which *Normandie*, having been launched into the river, would be able to reach her fitting out berth in the land-locked Penhoët Basin.

Completed in 1932 this structure, amongst the largest of its kind in the world, was officially named the Forme Ecluse Louis Joubert, after the then President of the Saint-Nazaire Chamber of Commerce: however, because of its intimate association with so famous a ship many would come to know it simply as the 'Normandie' dock.

Truly massive by the standards of the day, it was 350m long, 50m wide and 16m deep. Capped at each end by hollow 1,500 ton steel caissons, which could be wound in and out of sockets set into the western quayside, it had the very great advantage of being able to act as passage lock or dry dock as required. Capable of housing ships of up to 85,000 tons, the vast enclosure could be filled in only fourteen hours by powerful impeller pumps hidden deep beneath the Pumping Station next to the southernmost winding house. Considering the ease with which it could accommodate the most powerful warships then known, the 'Normandie' dock's strategic location and scale gave it an obvious military value; however, the more sinister implications of this were yet to be discerned in a world drifting only slowly towards war.

On 29 October, 1932, *Normandie* was launched to the strains of La Marseillaise and towed through the great dock to begin the lengthy process of fitting out. In the event her transformation into the ship whose honour it would be to win for France the Blue Riband for the fastest passage between Old World and New, was to take two and a half years; and it was not until 5 May, 1935, that she was ready to meet her element as the last word in elegance, the most beautiful ship afloat.

With Captain René Pugnet as master, she returned through the Forme Ecluse and, escorted by the destroyers *Adroit* and *Foudroyant*, made her way along the narrow channel which wound its way through the treacherous estuary shoals. As she slipped past the cheering multitudes who had come to bid her Godspeed, her departure was attended by ceremony such as would not be seen again until it was time for the new *Queen Mary* to make the same triumphant passage almost seventy years into the future.

Having been, for so many years, the pride of Saint-Nazaire, the departure of both great ships, despite their separation in years, would precipitate the same emotional void and the same fears for the continued employment of the multiplicity of skills which had contributed to their speed and beauty. However, while the new *Queen Mary* stands at the threshold of a working career likely to encompass some forty years of peaceful service, *Normandie's* days of glory were already numbered by the ignoble fate awaiting her in the distant Hudson River*: and as for all those who had come to cheer her passage, who amongst the throng could possibly have foreseen the crushing, demoralizing occupation that would all too soon follow defeat in war – still less the bloody battle which, in March of 1942, would play itself out amidst the very quays and jetties where they had stood at the moment of their city's greatest triumph.

* In December, 1941, *Normandie* was seized by the US Government, to be refitted as the troopship USS *Lafayette*. On 9 February 1942 – just a matter of weeks before the British would seek to destroy the great dock constructed for her in Saint-Nazaire – she mysteriously caught fire during coversion, capsizing in the Husdon river the following day. Eventually refloated in 1943 the hulk of this, the world's most beautiful ship, was put up for sale as scrap.

Chapter One

FESTUNG SAINT-NAZAIRE

Already renowned for its extensive dockyard facilities, Saint-Nazaire in the immediate pre-war years could also boast an enviable strategic position on the French Atlantic seaboard, daunting natural defences and a confidence-inspiring remoteness from the likely point of any German attack in the west.

The British had long recognized its many advantages as an access point for combatant forces wishing to enter France, troops having been fed through the port in 1914, en route to the Western Front. Later in the First World War the Americans had followed the British lead in disembarking expeditionary forces at Saint-Nazaire, an event commemorated by the impressive Mémorial Américain, a tall, bronze statue standing close by the Boulevard du Président Wilson, which shows a doughboy being carried onward by an eagle.

In the early months of the Second World War, Saint-Nazaire was again employed as a port of disembarkation for the BEF, the first

Debarkation of the 42nd (Rainbow) Division at Saint-Nazaire, 1 November 1917. Bay of Biscay ports were conveniently situated to facilitate access to the Western Front.

troopships arriving on 12 September 1939, following which a steady flow of convoys would continue to feed men and materiel into lines of communication stretching all the way to the battlefront in Northern France.

Deriving a spurious sense of security from the inactivity surrounding the 'Phoney War', and with their great distance from the German border appearing to render them immune from direct involvement in the conflict, the 36,000 inhabitants of Saint-Nazaire at first expected to suffer no greater hardships than tedium, confusion and concern for their loved ones mouldering at the front. Throughout the country complacency and indecision were the order of the day, the creeping sense of drift bringing with it a lassitude so comprehensive that defeat, when it finally came, was all the more shocking and complete – a fast-developing saga of despair and humiliation soon to consume the soul of one nation and lay siege to that of another.

Out-thought and outmanoeuvred, the French and British Armies were faced, in June 1940, with a tide of steel sweeping westwards from the Ardennes. Enacting a daring strategy of feinting in the north while delivering an armoured knockout blow against the French divisions which held the Allied Centre, this unstoppable German thrust across the Meuse was designed to trap the best of the Allied divisions in a Low Countries pocket within which they could be destroyed piecemeal.

The initial assaults took place on 10 May, the German strategy unfolding with such speed that by the 20th the tanks of General Heinz Guderian's Armoured Corps had reached the Channel coast, leaving the British with no alternative but to evacuate their surrounded forces by sea. Between 27 May and 4 June, the resolute prosecution of Operation DYNAMO resulted in some 338,000 men, including 220,000 of the BEF, being plucked from the port and beaches of Dunkirk.

To British civilian eyes the success of this mass evacuation seemed to signal the end of their direct involvement in the battle for France. Yet the truth was very different: for even as the last of the Dunkirk evacuees reached the safety of home, almost 200,000 British troops remained elsewhere in France – some securing lines of communication, other formations, such as the 1st Armoured and 51st [Highland] Divisions, continuing to fight alongside their French allies. These were to remain in place in support of the prevailing strategy which was to rearm the Dunkirk evacuees, return them to France and reconstitute the BEF in the west. In pursuit of this planned realignment of forces, supplies poured into western ports, the hinterland of Saint-Nazaire continuing to sprout massive new dumps of materiel.

Unfortunately, however, the strategy of the day proved to be no less unpredictable than the military situation. On 5 June, German forces launched a major assault against French and British forces established along the line of the Somme, their successful breakthrough only accelerating the inexorable chronology of defeat. On 12 June, some 40,000 Allied troops were forced to surrender to Rommel's armour at St Valery-en-Caux. On the 14th, Paris was occupied; and against this background of military and political meltdown the British finally abandoned all thoughts of reconstituting the BEF, deciding instead to save what they could of their surviving formations. On 15 June, the embarkation of troops began in earnest at Cherbourg, St Malo, Brest, Saint-Nazaire, Nantes and La Pallice.

The war had come at last to remote Brittany, whose roads were now packed with refugees and retreating troops. In Saint-Nazaire the population, numbed by defeat and uncertainty, looked on as most of the petrol and ammunition dumps so recently established were blown up one by one. Soldiers and civilians, British and French, men and

British soldier belonging to a specially formed destruction unit takes a pick to boxes containing petrol cans.

Vehicles that could not be taken on board ships were set on fire.

17 June 1940, soldiers and civilians queuing on the quayside at St-Nazaire to board a ship for England.

Left: The *Lancastria* under full steam.

Below: After being attacked by dive-bombers the *Lancastria* heels over with her propellers above the water.

women alike, scrambled for places on board the liners provided by the C-in-C Western Approaches. One of these, the unfortunate *Lancastria*, was bombed and sunk in the estuary of the Loire while packed with troops and refugees, news of the loss of 3,500 souls being temporarily withheld lest it affect adversely morale at home.

By 19 June, 57,000 troops had been evacuated through the ports of Saint-Nazaire and nearby Nantes, their departure characterized by disorganization and a fear of approaching German forces which sometimes bordered on panic. Disorder ruled the day, one unpalatable consequence being that huge quantities of newly arrived supplies were simply left behind on the dockside. Standing against these last, dispiriting manoeuvres was, however, the daring escape of the battleship *Jean Bart*, a product of Saint-Nazaire's own yards which, though incomplete, had been hurriedly readied for sea. With her guns not yet mounted and scaffolding still on board, she slipped out of port during the night of the 19th, her captain, Commandant Ronarc'H sailing her towards the safety of French North Africa.

Having narrowly escaped the attentions of the Luftwaffe, *Jean Bart* arrived in Casablanca on 22 June, the same day the Germans entered Saint-Nazaire, bringing with them a new and altogether more menacing incarnation for the port of her birth. For while the British might have seen in the Atlantic coastline the prospect of unimpeded access to the heart of France, the Germans chose to view it as a treasure-trove of easily fortified bases from which their surface ships and U-Boats could operate free from the risks inherent in passages to and from their home ports. Always assuming the war was not concluded quickly, Dönitz in particular would be able to exploit their natural advantages to the full, sailing his 'grey wolves' to savage allied shipping, thus to bring the recalcitrant British quickly to their knees.

During the halcyon months which followed victory in France, the U-Boats resumed the offensive which Dönitz had suspended in April to allow his boats to support the attack on Norway, his captains sinking a total of sixty-three ships in June alone. In response to Britain's refusal to capitulate, Germany tightened the screw even further by establishing an 'operational area' around the embattled islands, within which all ships were liable to be sunk without warning. Taken in conjunction with the shelving of invasion plans, this action finally freed the *Kriegsmarine* fully to concentrate on a crusade against the convoys bringing succour to the enemy. Over succeeding months a series of powerful warships would sail on extended anti-shipping cruises and achieve a certain success: however, as killing machines they and their great guns would prove no match for Dönitz, his fleet of unglamorous, yet cost-effective U-Boats and the chain of massive bombproof shelters even now being planned for their protection in each of the new Atlantic bases.

Designed by the Naval Construction Department of the *Oberkommando der Kriegsmarine* [*OKM*], these gargantuan reinforced concrete structures were marvels of packaging intended not only to protect the U-Flotillas, but to provide them with the full spectrum of logistical and engineering support. Their incredible complexity was described by Jerome M O'Connor, who in his article 'Into the Gray Wolves' Den', wrote that they were;

> *more like complete naval bases under concrete. Feeding the unquenchable needs of repair and overhaul facilities, underground pipes delivered oil, gasoline, lubricants, fresh water and seawater. All the necessities and many of the conveniences equivalent to a medium-sized town lay behind solid eleven-foot-thick reinforced concrete external walls and three-foot-deep steel armored double blast doors. Extending hundreds of feet within the immense interiors were complete steam and electric generating stations, air raid shelters, 1,000-man-capacity crew dormitories, cold storage and food lockers, mess facilities and scores of drafting and engineering offices. Other spaces contained fire-fighting, repair and first-aid stations, supply and storage rooms, kitchens, bakeries and hospital and dental facilities. Separate bunkers housed electrical transformers, fuel tanks and stand-by power generators. Dangerous or delicate stores, such as torpedoes, ammunition and optical instruments, went to fortified bunkers in town.*
>
> (Reprinted from NAVAL HISTORY with permission;
> Copyright © 2000 US Naval Institute/*www.navalinstitute.org*)

The shelter complex designed for Saint-Nazaire had room for twenty boats distributed through fourteen individual pens. Of these, pens one through eight could, when closed off by submersible caissons, fulfil the role of dry docks; while 'wet' pens nine through fourteen could hold two boats apiece. Measuring 299m in length, the fully completed shelter would be 124m deep and tower 18m high. Ultimately consuming almost 500,000 cubic metres of reinforced concrete, its extraordinary strength would ensure that it remained one of the few symbols of the 'Thousand Year Reich' likely ever to fulfil its temporal promise.

Surveys undertaken in 1940 led to a site being chosen on the western edge of the Saint-Nazaire Basin, close to the original railway station and obliterating the dock once used by the *Compagnie Générale*

U-Boat pens at St-Nazaire under construction. They would prove impervious to Allied bombs until the final year of the war when 22,000 lb 'Grand Slam' bombs could be dropped by RAF Lancasters.

Transatlantique. Strategically sound, this site was also of great moral value to the occupying forces, the shelter's impressive physical presence dominating wartime Saint-Nazaire just as it continues to dominate both port and town today.

Supervised by the Organization Todt's *Einsatzgruppe West*, work began in March 1941, the huge construction effort requiring a workforce of several thousand artisans and labourers. The initial effort was directed towards the completion of pens six through eight, these being declared officially 'open for business' on 30 June. The second *tranche* to be readied for use, pens nine through fourteen, were completed in January 1942 and in operation during the period when the British were preparing their sea-borne assault on the port. Paradoxically, given Britain's almost total dependence on the convoy lifelines to which the U-Boats presented by far the gravest threat, Bomber Command only began to attack the pens with conviction after they had been made essentially bombproof. As a consequence of their tardiness, many thousands of British and American bombs would eventually bring to Saint-Nazaire a devastation from which the targeted pens and their associated bunkers would be amongst the few

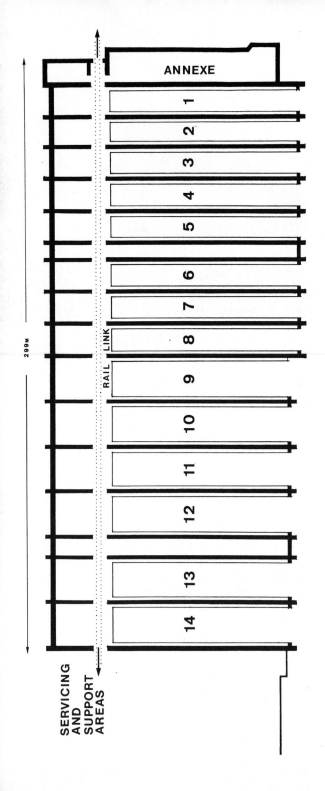

ANNEXE

1
2
3
4
5
6
7
8
9
10
11
12
13
14

RAIL LINK

299M

SERVICING
AND
SUPPORT
AREAS

U-BOAT PENS

SAINT — NAZAIRE

N

U-Boat at Saint-Nazaire with the roaring bull insignia of the 7th U-Flotilla painted on the conning tower.

structures to emerge completely intact.

In line with the completion of the first pens, June 1941 saw the arrival of the 7th U-Flotilla, commanded by *Korvettenkapitän* Herbert Sohler. Known as 'Flotilla Wegener', this flotilla, which sported the 'Bull of Scapa Flow' as its insignia, was to be associated with some of

Kapitänleutnant Topp conning *U-552* into pen 12 at Saint-Nazaire.
ECPAD/France DAM 1266

the most important boats of the war, these including *U-552* commanded by *Kapitänleutnant* Erich Topp, and *U-96*, whose commander, *Kapitänleutnant* Heinrich Lehmann-Willenbrock was portrayed by Jürgen Prochnow in the movie 'Das Boot'. In February 1942, *Korvettenkapitän* Wilhelm Schulz would bring the 6th Flotilla, named 'Hundius', to occupy the newly completed pens of phase two. By the time of their arrival, Saint-Nazaire's extensive militarization would be well into its stride, its combination of U-Flotillas, extensive dockyard repair and construction facilities and, in the mighty *Forme-Ecluse Joubert*, one of the largest dry docks in the world, fully justifying the port's new-found status as a target of deep and abiding interest to Britain's fighting and Intelligence services alike.

In recognition of their enemy's need to do whatever was necessary to disrupt the smooth functioning of such an important base, the development of new operational facilities went hand in hand with the construction, or revamping, of port and estuary defences. Within Saint-Nazaire itself, the virtually impregnable shelter complex became the hub of an increasingly sophisticated network of Flak defences. Quick-firing cannon of 20, 37 and 40mm calibres, in both single and multiple mountings, were placed on rooftops, Flak towers and bunkers, from which positions they could dominate local air space, the harbour approaches and the quays and basins of the port itself. Comprising three full battalions – the *703rd*, *705th* and *809th Marine-Flak-*

One of the four 75mm cannon of 1/MAA280 at la Pointe de St-Gildas.
ECPAD/France DAM 929 L 10

Inside the U-Boat pens at Saint-Nazaire.

Abteilungen – these made up the *22.Marine-Flak-Regiment* of *Kapitän-zur-See* Karl-Conrad Mecke.

Complementing this local defence was the coastal artillery of *Korvettenkapitän* Edo-Friedrich Dieckmann's *280th Marine-Artillerie-Abteilung* [MAA280]. Ranging in calibre from 75 to 240mm, his multiple batteries were emplaced along both shores of an estuary already made all but impassable by the extent of its deadly sandbanks and shoals. Directly overlooking the northern approaches and the deep-water Charpentiers Channel, were the *Batterie Behncke-West*, established on the heights of the Fort de l'Eve, the *Batterie Chémoulin*, close by Dieckmann's own HQ, and the *Batterie de Kermoisan*, at Batz-sur-Mer. Facing these positions, on the southern estuary shore, were the *Batterie Le Pointeau*, and the *Batterie St Gildas*. At an additional position, the *Batterie Préfailles*, it was planned to emplace powerful railway-mounted cannon to match the 240mm pair at Batz which had, as a prize of victory, been 'acquired' from the French Artillery Reserve.

Considering the degree to which the area's naturally restrictive geography complemented this extensive and interlocking network of gun defences, the *Seekommandant* [*Seeko*] Loire, *Kapitän-zur-See*

A 170mm gun position at the Fort de L'Eve. The bunker was designed to look like a house.

Adalbert Zuckschwerdt, might reasonably have concluded that all possible steps were being taken to make Saint-Nazaire secure. Certainly time was bringing with it mounting evidence of the RAF's new-found interest in bombarding the port from the air: but at least the sailors, gunners and technicians of its 5000-strong garrison could take comfort from the conviction, widely held, that not even the rash and unpredictable British would be mad enough to try and come up the river.

Chapter Two

A PLAGUE OF EMPIRES

One of the primary consequences of the World War at sea was a generational shift which saw the submarine and aircraft-carrier bring to a close that grand era during which mighty battleships had pounded one another to destruction for the right to rule the oceans.

Confirmation that the age-old heirarchy was now truly redundant arrived with the waves of Japanese aircraft which first devastated the US Pacific Fleet at Pearl Harbor, and then sank, off the coast of Malaya, the powerful British capital ships *Prince of Wales* and *Repulse*. In the southern hemisphere such tragedies succeeded in demonstrating only too clearly that the day of the 'dreadnought' was over: however, in northern waters the full implications of its passing would take rather longer to assimilate – especially given the power of the 'big-ship big-gun' lobbies in both British and German Admiralties.

Committed to war at too early a stage in its development, this fixation was perhaps most apparent in the *Kriegsmarine's* decision to use its heavy surface units as commerce raiders, a policy of desperation which only invited the piecemeal destruction of its most valuable assets. Particularly in the case of their battleships this was hugely wasteful of resources better committed to Dönitz's infinitely cheaper U-Boats: yet there was, in the sheer scale and potency of such ships a prestige so beguiling that, for so long as they remained operational, the British would have no choice but to pay almost any price in support of their destruction.

With this in mind, the foray of *Bismarck*, in May 1941, held within it both a present physical danger, as demonstrated by her summary destruction of HMS *Hood* in the Denmark Strait, and the seeds of a cancer which would continue to eat away at the very heart of British

The German battleship *Bismarck* photographed from the cruiser *Prinz Eugen* in May 1940.

naval strategy: for, even as the Royal Navy was engineering the crippling realignment of forces required to hunt this one ship down, her sister ship *Tirpitz* was working up in the Baltic prior to commencing her own portentous career.

Trailing a slick of oil from a lucky British hit, *Bismarck* was finally caught and sunk when almost within range of air cover. Celebrations were, however, blunted by the many questions surrounding the future deployment of her sister, most options holding within them the prospect of new humiliations. At the very least her malign presence in home waters would commit the British to a wasteful strategy of containment. Much worse was the possibility of her joining the battle-cruisers *Scharnhorst* and *Gneisenau* in Brest, as the lynch-pin of an immensely powerful German Atlantic Fleet.

Having succeeded in breaking the Enigma key in which the bulk of Germany's naval signals were encrypted, the code-breakers at Bletchley Park were able to follow *Tirpitz's* progress from the Baltic to Trondheim, where she arrived on 16 January 1942. The arrival of so potent a warship in Norwegian waters prompted an electric response in Britain, where all possible means were sought to discourage any ambitions she might have for a strike against the Atlantic convoys. Aerial reconnaissance provided a primary line of defence: others included Signals Intelligence, and the establishment, in home waters, of a naval force strong enough to defeat her should she ever be brought to battle.

In respect of influencing those whose responsibility it would ultimately be to decide on her future deployment, a final and rather

German battleship *Tirpitz*.

Kapitänleutnant **Herbert Kuppisch, CO of *U-94*, is subject of the kind of honour accorded to the U-Boat crews in the first flush of their success. Above and to the right is the Rue du Port. The Capitainerie is visible in the background, centre image.** ECPAD/FRANCE DAM 1171 L 06

desperate option was to deny *Tirpitz* the use of repair facilities which could be accessed directly from the Atlantic. Require her to run the gauntlet of waiting British forces in an attempt to reach the safety of a German port and the risks inherent in such an ambitious enterprise might well be increased beyond the margin of acceptability. In essence this would mean the neutralization of Saint-Nazaire's great 'Normandie' dock, the only structure on the whole Atlantic seaboard capable of housing so large a ship and the very facility for which the damaged *Bismarck* had been steaming when caught and sunk. But Saint-Nazaire had a sting in its tail; for this obvious target was already notorious for defences which appeared to render it invulnerable, having thus far defied all attempts to come up with a workable plan of attack.

On 26 January, Churchill met with the First Sea Lord, Admiral of the

Brigadier Charles Haydon, commander of the 'SS' ('Special Service') Brigade with Lieutenant Thomas Grenville Pitt 'Tom' Peyton, 6 Troop: 2 Commando, ML *192*. PETER COPLAND

Fleet Sir Dudley Pound, their conversation exploring the degree to which plans for *Tirpitz* might be affected by a successful strike against Saint-Nazaire. Adrift in a sea of speculation, their only dry land seemed to be the absolute certainty that for so long as the 'Normandie' dock remained available, the potential for new Atlantic dramas would continue to exercise a malign influence over the whole conduct of the war at sea.

Within twenty-four hours, the responsibility for divining a solution had been passed to the charismatic 'Adviser on Combined Operations', Commodore the Lord Louis Mountbatten, whose field of expertise was the planning and execution of sea-borne assaults on the enemy shore. Headquartered at 1A Richmond Terrace, in London, Combined Ops Headquarters [COHQ] had at its disposal the Army Commandos of Brigadier Charles Haydon's 'Special Service Brigade': however, with this one exception it commanded no forces, fleets or air armadas, relying for its effectiveness on the support and co-operation of the three traditional services. Unfortunately for the project now in hand such reliance was not always well rewarded: for the whole concept of 'combining' efforts was as yet quite foreign to an Army, Navy and Air Force acutely protective of their independent military identities.

Lord Louis Mountbatten

In contrast to this service self-interest, Mountbatten was at least able to benefit from the fruits of active Intelligence co-operation: for he was to find that an array of sources had already contributed to a mass of highly relevant material. In volume two of his book, *British Intelligence in the Second World War*, Professor F H Hinsley has written of how;

> *NID 1* [the Naval Intelligence Division], *with assistance from the ISTD* [Inter-Service Topographical Department], *compiled the shore information, some of which came from detailed plans of St Nazaire provided by the SIS* [Secret Intelligence Service – MI6]. *Information about the dock itself was obtained overtly from pre-war technical journals. Other information about shore defences, including coastal artillery,*

was provided by MI [Military Intelligence], with whom another section of NID now worked so closely on these topics as to constitute an inter-Service organisation. The OIC [Admiralty Operational Intelligence Centre] determined the approach route and the timing of the raid in the light of the Enigma intelligence about the enemy's swept channels and recognition signals, and AI's [Air Intelligence] knowledge of the GAF's [German Air Force] routine patrols. The CIU [RAF Central Interpretation Unit] supplied a special, detailed interpretation of photographs of the area and also the model that was used in the training of the raiding force.

(HMSO: Crown Copyright: p192)

A surprising quantity of detailed intelligence had come from French sources. Early in 1941 plans of the developing U-Boat base obtained by René Creston and delivered to Boris Vildé, leader of the resistance circuit within the Musée de l'Homme, in Paris, were passed on to London. Later that same year Henri Mouren, who worked in the naval shipyard at Saint-Nazaire, delivered a very special prize to Antoine Hugon, a Paris-based operative of Marie-Madeleine Fourcade's 'Alliance' network. Utilizing to the full the impact of an Iron Cross, worn on his lapel, which he had been awarded in the First World War for saving the life of a German soldier, Hugon made for her base in Pau, there undressing in the presence of astonished friends to reveal, wrapped around his torso, detailed plans of the port's new U-Boat complex. These too were quickly passed on to the British.

In the early stages of planning yet more intelligence would arrive

The 'Normandie' dock, looking towards the caisson rammed by HMS *Campbeltown*. The Pumping Station stands to the right of the caisson.

from France, this time by air in the form of Dispatch RZ 39, a package of information delivered by Gilbert Renault – better known, perhaps, as 'Colonel Rémy' – of the Gaullist 'Confrérie Notre-Dame' circuit, and providing even more up-to-date plans of the developing base.

The 'cloak and dagger' sourcing of so much germane material was reflected in the involvement of the Special Operations Executive, which maintained a liaison officer at COHQ, and was in direct contact with resistance circuits such as 'Alliance'. SOE had already investigated the possibility of blowing up the 'Normandie' dock using explosives placed by hand – indeed Joel Letac, an operative connected to its R/F section had gone so far as to volunteer for the job: however the quantity of explosives required far exceeded the maximum which could be put in place by agents on the ground. While this particular exercise might have come to nought, SOE would continue to play a pivotal role in Combined Ops planning, by contributing vital intelligence, by employing its specialist skills in the design and preparation of demolition charges, and by insinuating its own undercover operatives into the body of the attacking force.

With so much information already to hand, Combined Ops seemed to have everything but a solution to the problem of carrying a sizeable body of men through hundreds of miles of hostile waters and then insinuating them into 'Fortress Saint-Nazaire'. Yet almost before Mountbatten had time to pose this seemingly impenetrable question, he was to find that his planners had already identified an approaching alignment of sun, moon and earth which, during the last days of March, would cause exceptionally high tides to sweep across the estuary. Were a force to be assembled in time, then there just might be sufficient water over the shoals to allow vessels to pass which would otherwise be confined to the heavily defended deep-water channel.

The price for this approaching cosmic alignment was a timetable which allowed of zero flexibility. With this in mind proposals were produced as fast as they could be absorbed by empires as much concerned with protecting their own interests as with contributing to a successful outcome. In this the Admiralty would be most at fault for requiring that the job be done, while at the same time withholding such resources as would ensure that it be done well.

This perplexing dichotomy was demonstrated by the Navy's frosty response to Mountbatten's first plan. Largely the brainchild of his Naval Adviser, Captain John Hughes-Hallett RN, this involved only two destroyers, one of which, carrying a large explosive charge, would ram the outer caisson of the great dock and blow up after a suitable delay. A strong Commando force, carried on board both ships, would carry out a number of vital demolition tasks on shore following which survivors, plus the evacuated crew of the ramming ship, would re-embark on board the remaining destroyer. Assuming the attack was successful, a specially modified Motor Torpedo Boat would enter the dry dock and lay torpedoes against the structure of the inner caisson. Throughout the attack Bomber Command would stage raids designed to occupy the German gunners' attention. Put up to the Admiralty on 7 February, the plan was almost immediately dismissed. Under no circumstances could any of Britain's valuable destroyers be committed to such a hazardous enterprise: Mountbatten's team would simply have to find another way.

As February wore on and with time fast running out, it was Mountbatten himself who drew a veil over all speculation by threatening to cancel the enterprise unless a suitable ramming ship could be provided. Faced with such an ultimatum the Admiralty finally conceded defeat – at least insofar as providing as lead-ship for

The USS *Buchanan*, DD131: transferred to the Royal Navy in 1940, she was renamed HMS *Campbeltown*.

the raid a vessel already well past its prime. This, the obsolete American destroyer *Buchanan*, now sailing under British colours as HMS *Campbeltown*, was both a relic of the previous conflict and the sum total of the Admiralty's benificence. When she sailed to meet the enemy she would be supported only by light and highly flammable Fairmile Motor Launches, of all available vessels perhaps the ones least likely to survive the maelstrom of fire they were sure to meet in the estuary.

Throughout this period the COHQ planners had forged ahead with the assembly of forces and the development of the command structure most suited to this particular exercise. Reflecting the fact that it was a 'combined' operation, the decision was taken to appoint separate 'Naval' and 'Military' Force Commanders, who would work in concert through every stage of the execution of what was now to be known as Operation CHARIOT.

As Commander-in-Chief of the Coastal Sector from which the force would depart, Admiral of the Fleet Sir Charles Morton Forbes would act as 'patron' and exercise local control. The choice of Forbes was more a matter of protocol than preference, for he and Mountbatten had a 'history' dating from the period, in 1940, when Forbes had been C-in-C Home Fleet, and Mountbatten still a relatively junior officer in command of the troublesome destroyer *Kelly*. Faced with pressure to sanction the award of a DSO to Mountbatten for his 'success' in bringing *Kelly* home after being torpedoed, Forbes had demurred on the grounds that the young and somewhat accident-prone officer had blundered into a trap and was therefore entirely the architect of his own undoing.

Adding to an atmosphere already strained by battles with the Admiralty, the potential for conflict between CHARIOT's two most senior personalities did not bode well for a smooth passage into the final weeks of planning. Still worse was the growing suspicion that Bomber Command were less than fully committed to an operation in which they were meant to play a crucial role. During the early days of March their equivocation would centre on the provision of close air support. Other, more fundamental, reservations would emerge much later in the game.

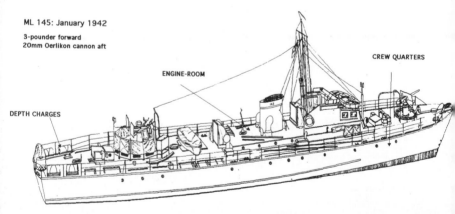

ML 145: January 1942

3-pounder forward
20mm Oerlikon cannon aft

CREW QUARTERS

ENGINE-ROOM

DEPTH CHARGES

COPYRIGHT JOHN LAMBERT

FAIRMILE 'B' TYPE MOTOR LAUNCH

Chapter Three

THE COMPANY OF KINGS

During the second week of March, *Tirpitz's* attempt to intercept the Russia-bound convoy PQ12, almost resulted in her being intercepted by the Home Fleet. Fortunate indeed to escape unscathed, her close shave only reinforced Hitler's conviction that his remaining capital ships would be better employed in deterring what he was certain were Churchill's ambitions in Norway. Taking into account the damage to the Reich's prestige which would be a certain consequence of her loss, she was therefore restricted to operations within the confines of the North Sea, sailing only when conditions did not threaten her survival, and when no British carriers were likely to be met.

Augustus Charles Newman

Robert Edward Dudley Ryder
LISLE RYDER

For those within the British Admiralty whose anxiety had been so greatly exercised by her move to Norway, this great ship's ineffective sally did little to justify their fears. How different might things have been had they only known that, with almost a month still to go before CHARIOT would seek to deny her the use of the 'Normandie' dock in distant Saint-Nazaire, it had also led to the worst of her sting having been drawn by her own side.

Attention at COHQ meanwhile shifted to the newly appointed senior ranks: to the Military Force Commander, Lieutenant Colonel Augustus Charles Newman, CO of 2 Commando, a territorial officer of thirty-seven; and to thirty-four year old Commander Robert Edward Dudley Ryder, RN, his Naval opposite number.

For the inspirational 'Colonel Charles', as Newman was known to his men, the key concern was the narrow envelope of time within which his Commandos would have to carry out a landing, then execute a daunting catalogue of demolitions on shore. With no support beyond the weapons and equipment they could carry, there would inevitably come a point beyond which engagement with a strengthening enemy could no longer be sustained. This being the case, he determined that all demolition tasks must be completed within thirty minutes of landing, and that re-embarkation should take place a mere ninety minutes after that.

Landing at three separate points in the dockyard, Newman's men would seek to isolate an operating area east of the South Entrance, the Saint-Nazaire Basin, and the lower portion of the Penhoët Basin. Assault troops would be first to storm ashore with the object of establishing a secure perimeter within which demolition troops could place their charges. Armed only with pistols and struggling forward under the dragging weight of heavy packs, these specialists would be given proximate cover by dedicated protection squads.

Captain Eric Stewart 'Bertie' Hodgson, 1 Troop, 2 Commando.
PETER COPLAND

Landing from six MLs at the heavily fortified Old Mole, Captain 'Bertie' Hodgson's GROUP ONE was tasked with seizing and holding the Mole itself, clearing the Avant Port and Old Town, destroying the Power Station complex and blowing all gates and bridges within the South Entrance. A little further to the north, another six MLs would put Captain 'Micky' Burn's GROUP TWO ashore in the deep indentation known as the Old Entrance. Burn's men, in conjunction with *Campbeltown's* parties, would seek to isolate the wedge of land between the two main basins and the 'Normandie' dock. For this purpose the Pont de la Douane [Bridge M], was to be destroyed and a blocking position established on the far side of the northern caisson. Storming ashore from *Campbeltown*, Major Bill Copland's GROUP THREE would complete the neutralization of the great dock by demolishing its Pumping Station, both winding houses and the northern caisson. A subsidiary task assigned to this group was the destruction of the underground fuel stores, immediately

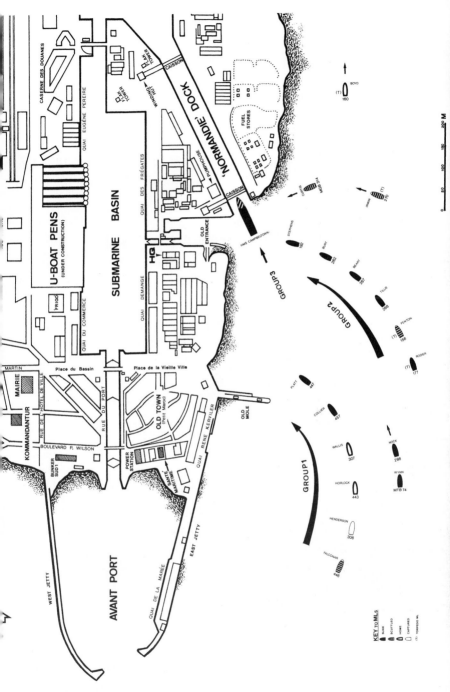

Plan of Attack, shown by group.

Major William Oranmore 'Bill' Copland, DSO, Second-in-Command. He was in charge of all Group 3 parties on the raid.
PETER COPLAND

east of *Campbeltown's* ramming point.

In preparing his men, Newman structured their training so as to reflect the very clear distinction between the demolition specialists and the fighting troops of the assault and protection parties. While much of the Special Service Brigade had contributed to the former group, the actual combat troops were sourced from Newman's own 2 Commando. When he was called to London, his second-in-command, Major Bill Copland, continued to push the selected few who would be expected to achieve so much amidst the darkness and mystery of Saint-Nazaire. Fortunately this crucial task could not have been left to a more capable officer; for when it came to extracting the best from the best, this forty-four year old veteran of Passchendaele possessed exactly the right mix of iron resolve and compassion.

As for the demolition troops, these had begun their training during the latter part of February in the Scottish port of Burntisland. Drawn from Nos 1, 2, 3, 4, 5, 6, 9 and 12 Commandos, their intensive instruction was left to Sapper Captains Bill Pritchard and Bob Montgomery – Royal Engineers who just happened to have planned for the destruction of the docks at Saint-Nazaire as part of an unrelated engineering exercise. Inspired by Pritchard, the men soon learned that even the most complex structures could be put out of action by well-placed explosive charges. As Major General Corran Purdon, at the time of the raid a young Lieutenant in 12 Commando, recalls;

> *we learned about caisson and double lock gates, winding houses, opening and closing machinery, steel bridges, cranes, guns, pumping stations and power stations. We were instructed in the use of plastic explosives and made-up charges, and where to place them in the most effective way and position. All of us became adept at the various means of iginition and the need for duplication. Bill Pritchard and Bob Montgomery made it all fascinating and our skill, speed and confidence increased rapidly.*

(Major General CWB Purdon, CBE.,MC.,CPM:
List the Bugle p26)

At the end of the month the men formed into two groups and moved south to continue their instruction in Cardiff and Southampton, with Pritchard supervising at Cardiff's Barry Docks, while Montgomery utilized to the full the many similarities between Southampton's huge King George V Dock and their target in Saint-Nazaire.

A father of four young children and with a fifth on the way, Newman's avuncular mein was very much in contrast to Ryder's apparent reserve. A dedicated regular officer, Ryder had served on warships, explored the Antarctic and commanded a number of vessels

Lieutenant Nigel Tibbits.
ANDREW TIBBITS

in his own right. Following the loss of his last ship to a collision he was acting as Naval Liaison to the headquarters of the Army's Southern Command, when called to take part in CHARIOT on 25 February, just three days after Newman's summons to London. Arriving in the capital on the 26th, he was late for the planning meeting and having missed an explanation of the raid's purpose, accepted the post of 'Naval Force Commander' without actually knowing who, or what force, he was to command.

Ryder quickly realized that he was expected to organize a major raid with no staff, no administrative structure and, at least until such time as *Campbeltown* belatedly appeared, no ramming ship. With so much at stake the allocation of the ageing destroyer added gravitas to a meeting, held on 3 March, which identified the Cornish port of Falmouth as the location from which the force would depart on the 27th, and Lieutenant Nigel Tibbits, RN, as the specialist who would take responsibility for transforming *Campbeltown* into a floating bomb. To expedite the modifications whose purpose would be to reduce her draft and give her the silhouette of a German vessel of similar class, the destroyer was to be sailed to the Devonport Naval Dockyard. To assist the force by confirming its point of entry into the shallows, a submarine would stand off the estuary mouth and show a light at the appropriate time. In line with the drift which was beginning to characterize Bomber Command's commitment, a request for close air suport was, however, refused.

On Friday 6 March, Ryder reported to Admiral Forbes' HQ in Plymouth. Having earlier failed on his own account to solve the myriad problems posed by targeting Saint-Nazaire, Forbes had already conveyed to Mountbatten his very real fear that in pushing ahead with such a risky operation, he was inviting the loss of most, if not all, of his men and ships.

At this stage the fleet consisted of *Campbeltown* and the twelve MLs which would share with her the burden of carrying Newman's Commandos, plus MGB *314* as headquarters ship, and MTB *74* – a heavily modified vessel whose powerful torpedoes would either supplement *Campbeltown's* charge or substitute for it should the

38

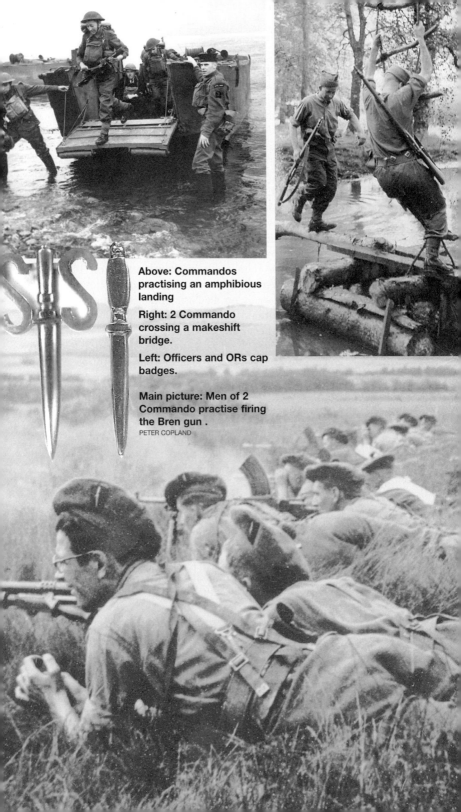

Above: Commandos practising an amphibious landing

Right: 2 Commando crossing a makeshift bridge.

Left: Officers and ORs cap badges.

Main picture: Men of 2 Commando practise firing the Bren gun .
PETER COPLAND

destroyer for any reason fail to reach the caisson.

The key naval personnel assembled in Forbes' HQ the following Tuesday. Lieutenant Commander 'Sam' Beattie, RN, had only recently been appointed to command *Campbeltown* and was learning of the raid for the first time. MGB *314* and MTB *74* were commanded, respectively, by Lieutenant Dunstan Curtis and Sub Lieutenant 'Micky' Wynn, both RNVR. The MLs were drawn from two Coastal Forces flotillas – the 20th, whose CO, Lieutenant Commander 'Billie' Stephens, RNVR, would act as Senior Officer MLs; and the 28th, led by Lieutenant Commander Wood, RN. Also attending were Lieutenant Bill Green, RN, as Force Navigator; the Signals Officer, Sub Lieutenant O'Rourke, RCNVR; and the pairing of Tibbits and Pritchard, who outlined their plans for the demolition of both *Campbeltown* and the enemy dockyard.

Having chosen the date for a rehearsal attack on Plymouth, consideration was given to the route they should follow to Saint-Nazaire. Determined largely on the basis of material supplied by Air Intelligence and the Admiralty's own Operational Intelligence Centre, this transpired to be a penetration deep into the Bay of Biscay, whose dual purpose was to guide the force away from enemy air patrols and frustrate any attempt to divine its true destination and purpose.

Following the discussions, Newman returned temporarily to London: Ryder, however, was free to move on to Falmouth there to establish the 'Tenth Anti-Submarine Striking Force', the spurious organization, with himself as Senior Officer, whose purpose was to cloak the assembly and training of CHARIOT forces and explain away both the installation of deck-mounted petrol tanks and the replacement of the MLs' feeble 3-pounder armament with 20mm Oerlikon cannon mounted forward and aft.

The MLs arrived in Falmouth on the 12th. Of the dozen plywood launches, four – MLs *192, 262, 267* and *268* – were drawn from Stephens' 20th Flotilla; while the remaining eight – MLs *298, 306, 307, 341, 443, 446, 447* and *457* – represented the full complement of Wood's 28th Flotilla. Designed for patrol and escort duty, these lightweight craft could hardly have been less suited to the role they were about to assume. Each would carry a squad of Commandos in addition to their own crews which, normally consisting of two officers and a dozen or so ratings, were supplemented by additional personnel for this one raid.

Having completed their training, the various demolition parties came together in Cardiff prior to entraining for Falmouth. At the same time, on the west coast of Scotland, the fighting troops of 2 Commando prepared to join them, sailing south from Ayr on board the troopship *Princess Josephine Charlotte* [PJC].

At last it was Newman's turn to leave the capital. As he exited COHQ, Mountbatten made it abundantly clear that as CHARIOT was an enormously risky operation, Newman should feel free to offer those with families, or with misgivings of a nature which might affect their performance on the night, the option of exclusion without prejudice to character. Oddly, considering the degree to which all present would share the same risks, this offer was not extended to the Commandos' naval comrades-in-arms.

His desire to have the most current aerial shots of the target area took Newman to RAF Medmenham, the home of the RAF's Central Interpretation Unit. The beautifully clear photographs showed an armed raider actually inside the 'Normandie' dock, as well as two new gun positions. Of the remainder of his journey to Falmouth he writes that:

> I stayed the night in Tavistock on the way down and remember how worrying it was to have a hotel bedroom full of the large model of St -Nazaire, and the latest aerial photos, four of the very latest wireless sets, and the orders in embryo for the raid. The lock to the bedroom wasn't a very good one, so my evening was a very uncomfortable one spent almost entirely in my bedroom!
>
> (Lieutenant Colonel A C Newman, VC: unpublished narrative)

The 'PJC' arrived in Falmouth on the 13th with the men of 2 Commando on board. As the loading of stores began, they were joined

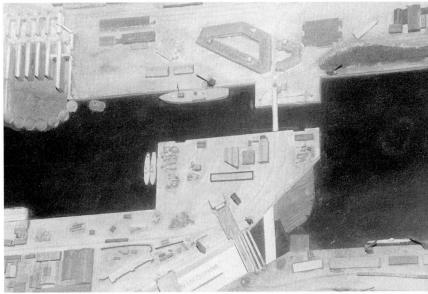

The northern segment of the RAF model used for the raid planning. In view is the junction between the Saint-Nazaire and Penhoët Basins, Bridge M and the Caserne des Douanes.

first by the demolition parties then, on the 14th, by Newman. The 14th also saw the arrival in port of the sleek, but skittish, MTB. Having originally been modified to attack *Scharnhorst* and *Gneisenau* in Brest, her motorless, explosive-packed torpedoes were now to be fired at the 'Normandie' caissons should *Campbeltown* ground or be sunk.

On the 16th the Commandos, distributed amongst the MLs, set off for a shakedown cruise out into the Atlantic. Initially intended to be a melding exercise, the whole affair was curtailed by a gale which forced the fleet to seek the shelter of the Scilly Isles. Many were violently seasick and the lesson was painfully learned that an attack in other than relatively benign conditions would be foolhardy at best.

Over the passage of weeks, Newman's force expanded steadily, the new personnel including Messers Gordon Holman and Edward Gilling, journalists from the *Exchange Telegraph* who were to report their first-hand experiences of a Commando assault. Holman was allocated to the gunboat, and Gilling attached to ML *307*, scheduled to land a small demolition team at the Mole. The gunboat would also host Captain Tony Terry, from Military Intelligence, and Private Peter Walker, nominally of 2 Commando. In fact 'Walker' was a Sudeten German whose real name was Peter Nagle and who was now an interpreter on the strength of SOE. The fact that Saint-Nazaire would be full of frightened civilians, prompted the inclusion of French-speaking personnel. For this purpose, Captain D R de Jonghe and Second Lieutenant J W R Lee, would travel on MLs *446* and *447* respectively. As was the case with Nagle, all was not quite as it appeared; for Lee was in fact the French national Raymond Couraud who, having crossed the Pyrenees to arrive in Britain the previous

HMS *Tynedale*. This destroyer, along with HMS *Atherstone*, would escort the raiders to the target. I.W.M. FL1676

October, had also joined SOE.

In respect of the weapons available, it soon became obvious that some sort of additional strike capability was needed lest the whole operation be put at risk by last-minute encounters with enemy vessels. The force would sail to Saint-Nazaire with the Hunt Class destroyers HMS *Tynedale* and HMS *Atherstone* as passage escorts; but as these were under orders to remain out of range of shore batteries, they would be in no position to assist when *Campbeltown* and the launches were at their most vulnerable. Cue Forbes, who in one of many demonstrations of his willingness to assist, allocated four torpedo-armed MLs from the 7th Flotilla, in Dartmouth.

With the gale-tossed Commandos back on board the 'PJC', Newman met with his thirty-nine officers and, in company with Ryder, revealed everything about their joint plan except the actual name of the target. They came together on the 18th in the electric atmosphere of the troopship's wardroom, and as the scale of the enterprise began to sink in, the sense of mission was palpable. Captain Micky Burn was seated next to his two subalterns, Lieutenant Tom Peyton and Second Lieutenant Morgan Jenkins – Tom, a product of Eton and Sandhurst; elegant, patrician: Morgan, Welsh-born, raised from the ranks, remembered by Micky as; 'our Richard Burton, with an all-conquering smile...my first experience, once or twice matched, but never surpassed, of Celtic charm.' Of that precious moment, the watershed between hope and fulfilment, Micky recalls that:

> *Tom and Morgan were sitting beside me. As Charles unfolded the plan, illustrating our separate tasks on a beautifully constructed model of the port, I heard Tom gasp with excitement at its audacity.... Dismally baulked as T E Lawrences in Norway* [where they had fought with the Independent Companies], *we were now to become Elizabethans. It would succeed [Charles] told us, because the Germans would think it impossible. At the end he asked if anyone had questions. I sent him a note: "Please may I go back to my unit?" He read it out. People laughed, tension relaxed and we dispersed with copies of the orders...* (Michael Burn, MC: *Turned Towards the Sun* p128)

On the following day it was the turn of the main body to hear that they were about to embark on the kind of 'special service' the prospect of which had encouraged them to volunteer for the Commandos in the first place. The tightness of the personal bonds which so characterized this elite formation, were reflected in their reaction to Newman's offer of exclusion without cost to their personal standing. Given the opportunity to leave prior to the disclosure of the plan, all personal

HMS *Campbeltown* showing Aft Deckhouse and 20mm Oerlikon positions seven and eight. LISLE RYDER

HMS *Campbeltown* showing midships gun platform, capped funnels and armoured deck screens. LISLE RYDER

doubts, fears and premonitions were brushed beneath the blanket response: 'Forget it! that's what we're here for!'

Having been joined by the gunboat and the half flotilla from Dartmouth – MLs *156, 160, 177* and *270* – Ryder's full complement of 'little ships' was available for VIVID the rehearsal scheduled for the night of 21-22 March. Conducted under the pretext of an exercise to test the defences of Plymouth and Devonport, the whole affair transpired to be a disheartening shambles. The all-important radios refused to work and blinding searchlights, allied to a spirited defence on the part of the forewarned Home Guard, meant that troops were either landed in the wrong place, or not at all. Forbes was observing from the roof of a shed, and was not at all impressed.

Ryder transferred his HQ to *Atherstone* when she and *Tynedale* arrived on the 23rd. It was now time for him to begin the briefing of his fleet's COs and First Lieutenants on board the 'PJC', using the scale model of the port to help identify features and structures. Amongst those who recognized the as yet unnamed target as Saint-Nazaire, was Sub Lieutenant John May, RNVR, the 'Number One' of ML *446*, who surmised that; 'either the Chiefs of Staff had gone crazy or the situation in the Atlantic was a great deal more desperate than we imagined.'

As the departure date loomed ever closer, Bomber Command's committment continued to dwindle, from a desired 350 or so aircraft, to a mere 62. To further complicate matters the stipulation that aircraft concentrate on areas of the town adjacent to the landing points, had fallen foul of a political decision aimed an minimizing French civilian casualties. On the 24th, Brigadier Haydon made clear his view that their air support was now both too weak to be effective and targeted in such a way as to invite the enemy's attention rather than divert it.

Thankfully unaware that their futures were still pawns in a game of political chess, the men of CHARIOT made their wills and wrote poignant 'last' letters to loved ones. It was a time whose deep emotion spills from the lines penned by 'Major Bill' on the 24th, to be read by his wife Ethel, in the event of his loss:

My dearest, I have to write this letter although God knows I hope you never receive it – which you will only if I don't come back. We sail in a day or two on a somewhat desperate venture, but one full of high purpose. If we succeed, and only the worst of ill luck will stop us, then we shall have struck a great blow for the cause of freedom. Remember too that if I do get blotted out I shall probably die in good company – for never did a finer crowd set out on a doughtier task. I shall always believe that Commandos are the real spirit of Britain at her best.

(Major WO Copland, DSO)

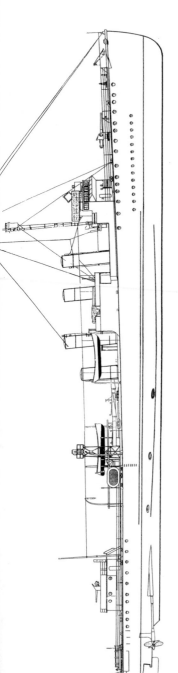

ORIGINAL CONFIGURATION

HMS CAMPBELTOWN

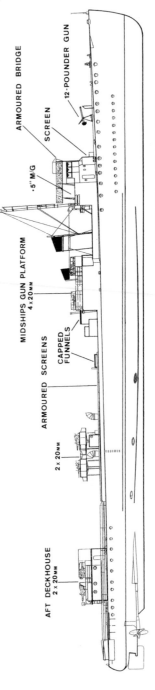

AS MODIFIED FOR 'CHARIOT'

ARMOURED BRIDGE

SCREEN

12-POUNDER GUN

·5" M/G

MIDSHIPS GUN PLATFORM
4×20MM

CAPPED
FUNNELS

ARMOURED SCREENS

2 × 20MM

AFT DECKHOUSE
2 × 20MM

On the 25th, *Campbeltown* finally steamed into harbour. With two of her four funnels removed and the remaining two cut back at an angle, she now had the silhouette of an enemy *Möwe* class boat. Gone was her main armament of 4″ guns, instead of which she now mounted eight 20mm Oerlikon cannon – four on each flank – and a solitary 12-pounder forward. Her bridge had been reinforced with armour plating, in addition to which armoured screens had been secured to the after deck to provide cover for those Commandos detailed to lie in the open during her final approach. At her heart was a huge explosive charge consisting of twenty-four depth charges concealed in a special tank built into her bow immediately abaft the forward gun support. Containing four and a quarter tons of Amatol, this was fitted with a variety of fuze types, the idea being to make absolutely sure of an explosion whatever the circumstances on the night.

With his whole force now assembled and so as to take advantage of a rare spell of settled weather, Ryder obtained permission to sail on the 26th, one full day ahead of schedule. The only fly in the ointment was the unwelcome appearance, in the most recent set of aerial photos, of five German torpedo boats [effectively light destroyers] tied up in the Saint-Nazaire Basin. As they substantially out-gunned the MLs, their presence in such a sensitive position did not bode well for the small ships' chances of survival. But there was little that could be done now, so the decision to sail was amended only by an appeal for such naval

HMS *Campbeltown*: midships gun platform, showing Oerlikon positions one through four. LISLE RYDER

reinforcements as could be made available so very late in the game.

On the morning of the 26th, a total of 269 men, made up of Newman's Commando force and its later accretion of odds and sods, transferred to *Campbeltown* and the various troop-carrying MLs. Observing everything with a journalist's eye was Gordon Holman, to whom the sheer quantity of stores and ammunition being loaded was more suggestive of an invasion than a raid. How could such a modest force need so much? The answer to that particular question would lie in the ferocity of their enemy's response.

At 1230 hrs, the receipt of Forbes' executive order, 'Carry Out CHARIOT', signalled the start of what many still viewed as a great adventure. The fleet made ready to sail – but without Lieutenant Commander Wood, who had been struck down at the very last minute by acute appendicitis. Having been an integral part of the planning process, Wood was to have led the port column of launches in their assault on the Old Mole, and there was no avoiding the fact that his loss would have an adverse effect on the balance of Ryder's command. As it was by now too late to find a suitable replacement on shore, there would be no alternative but to engineer a reassignment of duties even as the fleet was on its way to Saint-Nazaire

Chapter Four

WAITING TO EXCEL

Commander Ryder's impressions of this last-minute blow were recorded shortly after the raid.

We sailed at 1400 on the 26th March. With so many small ships, I found that there was always some last minute hitch to delay them. Sure enough, my last shock came at 1345, Lieutenant Commander Wood went sick. No officer is, of course, indispensable, but Wood was commanding the port column and had been one of my principal collaborators. If Wood led his column to the right landing place all would be well. The loss...at this stage, as can well be imagined, was a heavy blow. There was no time to do anything, the flotilla sailed with no one in command, and it was not till we were out to sea that we transferred Lieutenant Platt, RNR, the next senior, to the leading craft [ML447]. We had fortunately brought with us Lieutenant Horlock, RNVR, as a spare Commanding officer and so he was transferred to [ML443] in the place of Platt, and the force continued.

(Captain R E D Ryder, VC, RN: unpublished narrative)

Having cleared the harbour, the ships bore south-west for Position 'A', the first of a series of markers defining their route. While the MLs were capable of making the long trip under their own steam, the gunboat and MTB were both being towed, the former by *Atherstone* – currently home to Ryder and Newman – and the latter by *Campbeltown*.

Ahead of the fleet lay a journey of some 420 miles, scheduled to last for thirty-five hours at a mean speed of twelve knots. From Point 'A' the route would follow the six degree line of longitude until 170 miles west of Saint-Nazaire, at which point the fleet would turn south of east in the general direction of la Rochelle. Although Brest would be passed during the hours of darkness, discovery was likely at some stage, in which case great reliance would be placed on promoting the subterfuge of an anti-submarine sweep.

The early stages of the voyage were characterized by humour, imperturbability, even swank, a catalogue of emotions which served to camouflage the deep sense of loss engendered by the receding coastline of home. In his book *Commando Attack*, Gordon Holman describes how some of the Commandos were less than convincing in their claims to be 'getting their sea-legs', having given in to the swell

HMS *Campbeltown* showing the signal platform on the starboard side. Visible is the .5 inch Browning machine gun. Ordnance Artificer Frank Wherrell, RN, is standing immediately forward of the signal locker, in overalls and cap. LYLE RYDER

without much of a fight. The comment of one sufferer, to the effect that: 'If I had wanted to be a... sailor, I wouldn't have joined the... army!' succeeded in capturing the mood of more than a few uncertain 'Pongos'.

Of the situation on board *Campbeltown*, which was carrying the various parties of GROUP 3, 'Major Bill' Copland recalls how:

All that afternoon and evening we sailed under perfect weather conditions, calm with a sunshine haze which helped to reduce enemy visibility. Aboard Campbeltown *all was ship-shape and comfortable – I had sent John Proctor* [Lieutenant, 5 Troop: 2 Commando] *aboard early in the day to fix and allocate quarters – and soon everyone was snugly settled in. There was little to do, all our preparations had been made on 'PJC' and it only remained to arrange our tours of duty for AA defence, rehearse "Action Stations" and wait. Troops and sailors were very quickly "buddies" and as no khaki was allowed to be seen on deck – the limited number who were allowed*

up...appeared in motley naval garb – anything from oilskins to
dufflecoats, not forgetting Lieutenant Burtinshaw [Lt R J G, 5
Commando] *who discovered one of Beattie's old naval caps and*
wore it during the whole voyage. During this first day too, we
allocated all our landing ladders and ropes in places on deck
where we thought they would be most wanted. Gough [Lt
Christopher, RN, Beattie's "Number One"], *was to be in*
charge of all tying-up and ladder control and his help in the
allocation was invaluable.

(Major W O Copland, DSO: unpublished narrative)
As experienced from the bridge of *Atherstone*, Newman was able to
take a more contemplative view of the first day than Ryder, upon
whose shoulders lay the whole responsibility for bringing the force
safely to Saint-Nazaire. Writing of those first hours, he vividly recalls
that:

We, in the Atherstone, *the only military personnel, Stan*
Day, Tony Terry and I, were entertained and made very
comfortable by the officers and men of the crew. The rest of my
HQ troops were in the MGB which was being towed behind...to
save fuel.

The first part of the voyage we had been sailing in two
columns – line ahead, but later in the day as we neared the Brest
coast the Anti-Submarine Sweep formation was adopted – the
signalling of the altered sailing instructions being flagged from
the Atherstone, *picked up and answered by the MLs and then,*
when the last had answered and the signal flags [were] *struck,*
the fine sight of each vessel changing speed and direction to take
up its new position.

(Lieutenant Colonel A C Newman, VC: unpublished narrative)
At 1911, the force turned to port at Position 'A' and sailed south into the
gathering darkness. The fading light signalled the end of their air
cover and prompted the adoption of Ryder's night cruising order. Lest
they be seen and reported by fishing vessels, the German naval ensign
was hoisted.

On reaching Position 'B' at 2300 the 120 mile overnight leg was
begun which would bring them to the latitude of Saint-Nazaire by
morning. Their route towards Position 'C' would place the force astride
the U-Boats' main transit routes to and from the Atlantic. In the early
months of 1942 these were considered generally safe by U-Boat crews.
Certainly the crew of *U-Kelbling, Kapitänleutnant* Gerd Kelbling's U-
593, had no thoughts of running into the British as they made for Saint-
Nazaire at the conclusion of a terrifying first war patrol during which

they had been heavily depth-charged. Arriving at a position 160 miles west of Saint-Nazaire early on the morning of the 27th, a periscope sweep prior to surfacing betrayed the presence of destroyers and other small craft to the west; however, in an area effectively closed to Allied warships, these were at first taken to be friendly. Surfacing cautiously, *U-Kelbling* maintained its easterly course, all the while keeping a weather eye on the strange formation.

From the British perspective the fleet, having reached Position 'C', altered to port. Now steaming at eight knots, they should have appeared to any observer to be heading directly for La Rochelle. At 0710 *Tynedale*, which was flying the German ensign, spotted *U-593* to the north east, and she and *Atherstone* gave chase. In purely military terms the ensuing confrontation transpired to be a draw, with the U-Boat subjected to gun and depth-charge attacks, while she in turn made an abortive torpedo attack on *Tynedale*. However, in terms of its impact on the raid, the failure to do more than force the U-Boat to dive would later prove a blessing; for, having remained at 180m for some hours, Kelbling would later report the fleet as sailing west, away from the Biscay coast, instead of east, directly *towards* it. On receipt of his delayed signal '*0620* [0720 BST], *three destroyers, ten MTBs, forty-six degrees fifty-two minutes north, five degrees forty-eight minutes west: course west*', German 'Group Command West' would both conclude that the ships posed no immediate threat to the coast, and despatch to patrol the U-Boat approach routes, the five Torpedo Boats of *Korvettenkapitän* Moritz Schmidt's 5th Flotilla, the one formation which could so easily have scuppered the raid had they been met later in the estuary.

At the conclusion of the chase, circa 0930, *Tynedale* and *Atherstone* steamed away to rejoin the rest of the fleet, retiring to the south-west in case they were being observed. Having restored the gunboat's tow, Ryder had his ships on course again by 1100, making south of east for Position 'D'. For a time at least their way ahead seemed clear: however, as Ryder himslf recalls, it was not long before French fishing boats were met which just might carry radios or German observers. He therefore,

> ordered Tynedale *to investigate the trawler on the port side while we slipped MGB 314 and sent her to board the one close on her starboard side. She was instructed through the loud-hailer to take off the crew, search the ship for wireless equipment and bring off her log and any books, regulations, etc., that might be of use including her charts and route instructions. This she did in a swift and businesslike manner and very shortly both trawlers were sunk by gunfire.*

(Captain R E D Ryder, VC, RN: unpublished narrative)

As the day drew on, the question of whether or not they might meet the German Torpedo Boats was never far from Ryder's mind. At 1240 he received a signal from Forbes confirming the presence of the five ships in Nantes, as of the 25th, PM. This was not long before, far in the fleet's wake, Kelbling at last judged it safe to bring his boat to the surface and make his misleading sighting report. While this was not acted upon immediately it did nevertheless result in the flotilla being sent out into the Bay during the same envelope of time in which Ryder was first receiving the further intelligence that it had moved downriver and was once again in the proximity of his attack zone.

Far removed from the worries of command, there seemed to be as many different ways of dealing with the onward march of time as there

Waiting time – even colonels need to rest. Lieutenant Colonel Charles Newman with the padre and a pint in Scotland, 1941. PETER COPLAND

Lieutenant Stuart Chant.
LT COL IAN CHANT-SEMPILL

were sailor and Commando souls on board the fleet. Closed up at 'action stations' on the gunboat's forward gun, Able Seaman Frank 'Smudger' Smith, RN, recalls how:

The atmosphere on board was quite relaxed. Relations between the sailors and the Commandos were very good, much skylarking and bantering. To put in their time, the Commandos were cleaning their revolvers [sic] taking their Bren Guns apart, or sharpening their knives. I remember [some] of the Commandos trying to decide whether to land in pants or kilts. As we neared to the French coast, and our feelings on survival, I don't think I gave it a thought, at my age – nineteen that month. I think we all thought we were invincible.

(F A Smith, DSM: unpublished narrative)

In charge of the small demolition team whose job it would be to blow up the dock's all-important impeller pumps, Lieutenant Stuart Chant, relieved to be done with all the preparation, felt curiously light of heart at the thought of being at last committed to the enterprise. As with so many of the Commando officers, but particularly those in charge of demolition teams, he set his men to checking their equipment. Every one of the demolition specialists, officers and men alike, had been provided with an assemblage of pre-packaged explosives tailored to the specific requirements of each individual target. Contained in rucksacks which could weigh in excess of thirty kilos, their bulk was a function of the Commandos' paucity in numbers as set against the sheer scale and complexity of targets to be attacked. Designed and assembled at SOE Stations IX [The Frythe], and XII [Aston House], these were yet another product of the cooperation between the Commandos and their similarly venturesome SOE counterparts.

For *Campbeltown's* truncated crew there was much to be done. While the cooks dished up eggs, bacon, tinned fruit and fresh bread for which the Commandos were deeply and voraciously appreciative, those on watch in the engine-room did what they could to facilitate the scuttling

**Charles Newman,
Left, with his
adjutant Captain
Stanley Ambrose
Day, MC (centre).**
PETER COPLAND

AIRMILE TYPE 'C' MOTOR GUN BOAT

**(MGB 314 SHARED GENERAL LAYOUT
BUT WITH VICKERS 2-POUNDER
ON FOREDECK)**

ARMAMENT   2 POUNDER Q.F. MARK IIC GUN ON MARK XV (POWER) MOUNTING.
TWO TWIN .5" VICKERS MACHINE GUNS IN MARK V POWER MOUNTINGS.
2 POUNDER ROLLS ROYCE GUN ON MARK XVI MOUNTING.
PAD FOR HOLMAN PROJECTOR. (WEAPON NOT FITTED).
TWO TWIN .303" VICKERS G.O. MARK I MACHINE GUNS ON BRIDGE.*
FOUR DEPTH CHARGES.
TWO SMOKE FLOATS.
TYPE 286 SEARCH RADAR AT MASTHEAD.
                                                          *NOT SHOWN

Q 328

SCALE   0   10'   20'   30'   40'   50'   60'   70'   80'   90'   100'   110'
                                                                    FEET

COPYRIGHT JOHN LAMBERT

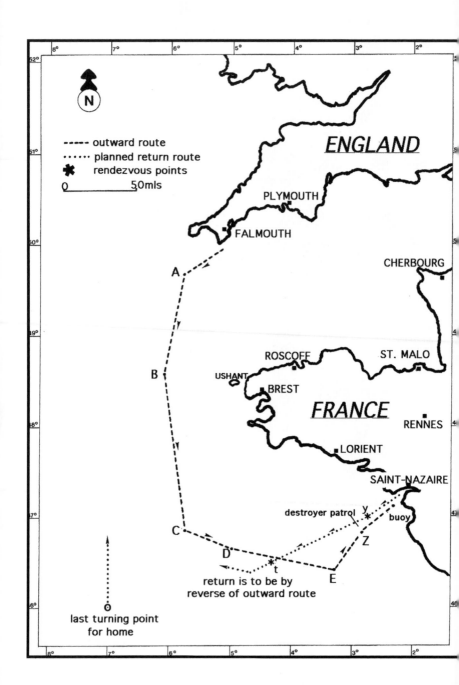

N

outward route
planned return route
rendezvous points

0   50mls

ENGLAND

PLYMOUTH
FALMOUTH

CHERBOURG

A

49°

ROSCOFF   ST. MALO

B   USHANT
BREST

FRANCE   RENNES

LORIENT

SAINT-NAZAIRE

destroyer patrol y   buoy
C   Z
D
t   E
return is to be by
reverse of outward route

O
last turning point
for home

of the ship immediately after ramming. In the knowledge that speed would be of the essence, every possible means for allowing water into the hull was prepared well in advance.

As part of the deception process aimed at maintaining security, *Campbeltown* had been provisioned as per normal for a two-way passage. It took a while for the penny to drop, but eventually the realization dawned that the ship was replete with goodies which would shortly go up in smoke were they not first 'liberated'. The result was a cathartic raid on the ship's stores; a redirection of pent-up energy into a comedy of consumption that would long be remembered by those who took part.

Private William Anthony 'Dutch' Holland, from the starboard side assault team, filled his pockets with cigarettes, as did his pal, Private John Gardner, their decidedly optimistic plan being to ensure a quiet smoke on the way home. Corporal Bob Hoyle, of Purdon's team, remembers how; 'someone brought a side of bacon and we poured mustard and sauce over that – made a great big pile of all the food.' The ship's Cook, nineteen year old Walter Rainbird, noticed the more prescient of the Commandos packing their booty into 'french letters' to protect it from the sea. And Corran Purdon recalls how some, 'made dreadful sandwiches containing such things as Brylcreem, shaving soap and toothpaste and offered them to unsuspecting friends'.

But there was, of course, another side to the coin as exemplified by Stuart Chant who, only too aware that fate must still demand a price of all who dare, would later have cause to remember with great sadness, how his close friend Lieutenant Robert Burtinshaw, of 5 Commando, sporting one of Beattie's naval caps, made a great pretence of assuming command of the ship. The wearer of a monocle, whose men had affectionately nicknamed him 'Bertie Bagwash', Burtinshaw's 'send up' of the Senior Service would transpire to be the last real memory many would have of him as he was numbered amongst the many all too shortly to sacrifice their lives

Within just two hours of having received Forbes' warning that Schmidt's flotilla was in the immediate area of the estuary, Ryder was informed that the two additional destroyers, *Cleveland* and *Brocklesby* had been sailed at maximum speed to reinforce the fleet – something they were now very unlikely to do in time for their guns to be of any use. This last signal was made just one hour before the fleet arrived at Position 'E', shook itself out into attack formation and, with all pretence now at an end, turned north-east directly for Saint-Nazaire.

Position 'E' was the point of no return. The fleet was now only seventy-five miles from target, looking out for the beacon shone from *Sturgeon* which would confirm their entry point into the estuary. The

CURTIS

MGB 314

IRWIN 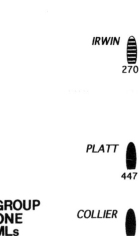 T
270

T BOYD
160

PLATT
447

HMS CAMPBELTOWN

STEPHENS
192

GROUP
ONE
MLs
(OLD MOLE)

COLLIER
457

GROUP
THREE
(CAISSON)

BURT
262

GROUP
TWO
MLs
(OLD ENTRANCE

WALLIS
307

BEART
267

HORLOCK
443

TILLIE
268

HENDERSON
306

T FENTON
156

FALCONAR
446

T  RODIER
177

NOCK

298

WYNN

MTB 74

ATTACK
FORMATION

rapidly fading light cast a veil over the myriad emotions which had characterized the long, last day. This was the time to focus and open minds to the potentialities which banter and skylarking had helped to banish to the outer reaches of consciousness. The enemy coast was ahead, Ryder writing that:

When evening came and there were still no signs of air attack, reconnaissance aircraft, or the Torpedo Boats, our spirits were high. It seemed incredible that we could really steam here in broad daylight without being spotted. Evidently, the submarine had decided to remain submerged until dark, perhaps he thought we would have his locality watched from the air. Perhaps he had reported us as two destroyers bound for Gibraltar. Anyhow, here we were, it was nearly dark and the sea oily calm. We stopped the force and, working to plan, Green, Newman and I transferred to the MGB and hauled out ahead of the force. Campbeltown *slipped MTB 74 which took station astern. As soon as we saw that this was completed, we signalled* Campbeltown *to steer a course to the north-east at fifteen knots.*

Our formation during the approach consisted of the small striking force of MGB 314 and two torpedo carrying MLs ahead, Campbeltown, *followed by the remaining MLs in two columns, MTB 74 bringing up the rear and the two escorts,* Atherstone *and* Tynedale *spread on either side to improve our chances of sighting our beaconing submarine.*

(Captain R E D Ryder, VC.,RN: unpublished narrative) Having enjoyed great good fortune up to this point, an incident now took place which would jeopardize the whole attack on the Mole. ML 341 reported engine trouble and was obliged to transfer her Commandos and return to the UK. To cope with just such an emergency two MLs had been included as spares. One of these, Lieutenant Falconar's ML 446, now came alongside and took on board the fourteen men of Captain 'Bertie' Hodgson's assault party, the medical team of Captain Barling – one of the two Commando doctors – and Captain de Jonghe. All of this took place while the main force sailed on into the night. Even at maximum speed there was now little chance of Falconar ever returning Hodgson to his rightful place in the formation, the consequence being that his all-important assault troops, instead of being in position to support the capture of the Old Mole, would now be unlikely to arrive until the struggle for it had already been decided, one way or the other.

ML 446, sparks erupting from her funnel, was still chasing the main body when, at 2200, *Sturgeon's* positioning beacon was sighted. As remembered by Corran Purdon:

> *It was an unforgettable moment when we saw the half-submerged submarine lying with the conning tower showing, the figure of her captain, Commander Wingfield, waving to us and shouting "Good luck!". We all admired the superb navigation by Lieutenant Green, in the MGB, which had brought us with amazing accuracy to this tiny rendezvous in the ocean.*
>
> (Major General C W B Purdon, CBE.,MC.,CPM: *List the Bugle*: p 31)

As the force of 'little ships' steamed through Position 'Z', and on towards the brooding darkness where lay the estuary mouth, it left behind both *Sturgeon,* and the two destroyers whose presence in the wings had thus far added a comforting solidity to their presence deep in enemy waters. In response to orders, *Tynedale* and *Atherstone* now broke away to establish a patrol line offshore as they waited for surviving boats to come out.

Her duty done, *Sturgeon* dived prior to heading north to patrol off Brest. As she slipped beneath the waves, Wingfield was unaware that her light had been spotted by the surging ML *446* which, anxious to know if the submarine was in the right position, passed close overhead, her frustrated bridge crew calling over the side: 'Come up, you silly buggers!'

Chapter Five

A WHISPER OF GHOSTS

The accuracy of its course having been confirmed by *Sturgeon's* light, the fleet made for the buoy which would guide them into the shoals. Having stuck rigidly to his timetable, Ryder could now be confident of passing this final marker close to the target time of 0030/28.

With midnight in the offing, Lieutenant Nigel Tibbits activated *Campbeltown's* huge charge, employing a variety of fuze types so as to guarantee an explosion irrespective of conditions on board the ship after ramming. In response to Ryder's demand for absolute certainty, he had,

> *Produced an underwater fuze with which he intended to blow up the ship two or more hours after sinking. [He] convinced us of the reliability of this method and produced also a proposal to use an Army "L-delay" fuze in addition. This would be set to a delay of eight to twelve hours and inserted in each charge before the ship entered the river. Twenty-four depth charges were going to be used and these would be watertight so that even if all the other underwater fuze leads were torn off, destroyed or damped*

HMS *Sturgeon*.

out, each depth charge would have in its middle a fuze already set to blow up after eight or twelve hours. This particular type of fuze apparently is not liable to detonate and so our fears on that account were also removed.

(Captain R E D Ryder, VC, RN: unpublished narrative)

The timing of all such fuzes, whether 'L-Delay', based on the stretching point of lead, 'AC Delay', based on the time taken for an acetone solution to eat through a cellulose disc, or the more commonly used 'Time Pencil', activated by a corrosive fluid eating through a steel wire, but unsuitable for use underwater, was notoriously unreliable. All three suffered from poor quality control which, when allied to an acute sensitivity to variations in temperature, could cause them to err by twenty percent or more. That the destroyer would explode eventually was never seriously in question: however, the long wait for a bang was to prove acutely unsettling for those left behind on the Saturday morning.

While some, such as Second Lieutenant Bill 'Tiger' Watson, in charge of the protection party on board ML 457, had chosen to sleep through these final manoeuvrings, many were on deck to hear the oncoming drone of their air support, and observe the dark sky to the north east suddenly dance with colour and light as the German defenders reacted to the ominous traces on their operators' radar screens.

In Saint-Nazaire the alert had been sounded at 2320, the wail of the sirens bringing to a state of readiness the doctors, nurses and stretcher-bearers of the civilian 'Défense Passive'. Also rushing to their action stations were the crews of the artillery pieces, searchlights and fire-control systems charged with protecting the port and its approaches.

Particularly relevant in respect of air attack were the light and medium *Flieger Abwehr Kanone*

Second Lieutenant Bill 'Tiger' Watson, 1 Troop, 2 Commando, ML 457.
DR W.H. WATSON

[Flak] of the three battalions comprising Mecke's *22. Marine-Flak-Regiment* – the dual-purpose cannon whose rapid fire would, if not directed elsewhere, have a devastating impact on Ryder's mostly wooden-hulled fleet.

Already both reduced in scale and redirected away from the areas where it would have had the most effect, the raid had been further emasculated by operational orders which prevented the crews from bombing below a certain height, or unless they could identify their targets precisely. In the event, a layer of cloud well below their permitted ceiling would ensure that only a handful of aircraft succeeded in dropping any bombs at all, the majority being forced to abort at exactly the point where Ryder's ships were most in need of their support.

Only too aware that the British were unlikely to send aircraft this far and then do nothing with them, Mecke's suspicions would prompt him to issue a warning that units be on the alert for parachutists. Having been included in CHARIOT for the purpose of keeping the enemy's attention 'diverted' the odd behaviour of the aircraft therefore only succeeded in alerting the Germans to the possibility that as they weren't dropping bombs, they must be serving some other malign, if as yet unidentified, purpose.

At 2345, by which time the ship's naval personnel were already at 'action stations' and all guns' crews 'closed up', Major Bill Copland brought his Commando officers together for a final briefing in *Campbeltown's* wardroom. In spite of the circumstances he recalls it as being; 'a calm, confident, cheerful gathering and the atmosphere, outwardly at all events, far from seeming electric, was quite ordinary.'

Present were a total of fourteen officers: Copland to be in overall control of the disembarkation and all action in and around the 'Normandie' dock; with Captain Bob Montgomery and Lieutenant Bill Etches overseeing all GROUP 3 demolitions ashore. Commanding the all-important assault parties were Captain Donald Roy, with Lieutenant Johnny Proctor, to port; and Lieutenant Johnny Roderick, with Second-Lieutenant John

Captain Donald Roy.
RODERRICK ROY

63

GROUP 3
CAMPBELTOWN PARTIES

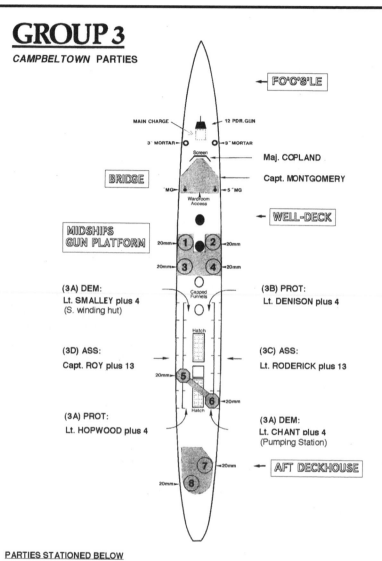

FO'C'S'LE

MAIN CHARGE   12 PDR. GUN

3" MORTAR   3" MORTAR

Screen

Maj. COPLAND

BRIDGE   Capt. MONTGOMERY

"MG   5"MG

Wardroom Access

WELL-DECK

MIDSHIPS GUN PLATFORM

20mm ① ② 20mm

20mm ③ ④ 20mm

(3A) DEM: Capped Funnels   (3B) PROT:
Lt. SMALLEY plus 4   Lt. DENISON plus 4
(S. winding hut)

Hatch

(3D) ASS: (3C) ASS:
Capt. ROY plus 13   Lt. RODERICK plus 13

20mm ⑤

⑥ 20mm

Hatch

(3A) PROT: (3A) DEM:
Lt. HOPWOOD plus 4   Lt. CHANT plus 4
(Pumping Station)

⑦ 20mm   AFT DECKHOUSE

20mm ⑧

PARTIES STATIONED BELOW

(3A) DEM: Lt. BURTINSHAW plus 7▪ (3B) DEM: Lt. BRETT plus 7 ▪ (3B) DEM: Lt. PURDON plus 4
(S.Caisson)   (N.Caisson)   (N.winding hut)

Stutchbury, to starboard. Tasked with destroying the north caisson, was Lieutenant Gerard Brett – Lieutenant Burtinshaw fulfilling the same task at the southern end of the dock, should it prove necessary. Lieutenant Corran Purdon's team would take care of the northernmost winding hut, while Lieutenant Chris Smalley's men blew its twin to the south. While all these demolitions were being carried out amidst the mayhem of fighting above ground, Lieutenant Chant's party would descend into the bowels of the Pumping Station and place charges on each of the four vital impeller pumps. As for protection, Lieutenant 'Bung' Denison would look after the northern demolition parties, and Lieutenant 'Hoppy' Hopwood, those operating in the immediate area of the ramming point.

Lieutenant 'Hoppy' Hopwood. PETER COPLAND

Copland having issued the order: 'Action Stations, please, gentlemen,' the gathering broke up around midnight. It was now time for the various parties to take up their allotted positions, either behind the meagre shelter of the deck-mounted armoured screens, or below, but within easy reach of a companion-way. So as to have an uninterrupted view during the final approach Copland chose to position himself next to a screen between the bridge structure and the navy-crewed 12-pounder gun. To right and left of his station would be two 3" mortars, commanded by Johnny Proctor.

The fleet reached the final positioning buoy at 0025/28. Shortly thereafter, and only a little way to port, there loomed the skeletal upperworks of the sunken *Lancastria*. As many of the Commandos had been evacuated from Norway on board the old 'Cunarder', the sight was a stark reminder of the pain and humiliation which had characterized the retreats of 1940: all the more so for Sergeant Tom Durrant, travelling on ML *306* as part of Lieutenant Ronnie Swayne's nine-man demolition party, his brother having won the Military Medal for his actions during her loss.

In the van of the formation the gunboat manoeuvred to take soundings. As with all the other small ships, its crew had been closed up at action stations for some time already. The after Rolls-Royce pom pom having packed up when Curtis cast off from *Atherstone* to intercept the fishing boats, MGB *314's* primary armament was now its forward 2-pounder Vickers pom pom, with its all-'brummie' crew of Able Seamen Frank 'Smudger' Smith as trainer, and bearded Bill

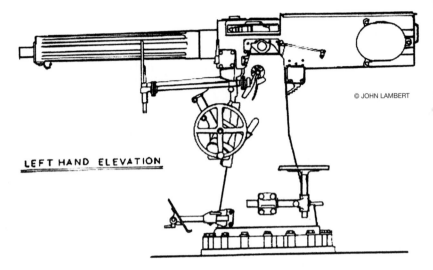

© JOHN LAMBERT

LEFT HAND ELEVATION

The Vickers 2-pounder Pom Pom.

Savage as layer. Controlling the fire of this gun was Sub-Lieutenant Chris Worsley who wryly recalls,

> *Lying flat on the deck beside the trainer's feet, behind a splinter-mat secured to the guard rails – that gave me at least the FEELING of protection!*

Positioned either side of the superstructure amidships were two powered machine-gun mountings. Operated hydraulically, these would prove just as susceptible to enemy fire as the similarly powered steering systems on board the MLs.

Penetration of the estuary proper occurred when the first ships approached the treacherous Banc du Chatelier. To the alarm of all those on board, *Campbeltown* grounded briefly before tearing herself free again. It was the first of two such contacts with the bottom, either of which – had it not been for the earlier reduction in speed designed to nullify her tendency to squat at the stern – might have made a gift of the old destroyer to the shore batteries which, still eerily silent, now all but surrounded them.

Such apparent disinterest a mere seven miles and forty-five minutes from target, spoke volumes for both the enemy's alertness and the brilliance of Hughes-Hallett's plan. Now well within range of no fewer than eighteen medium to heavy artillery pieces distributed through five well-chosen positions, the fleet should, by rights, have been in the centre of a deadly web of fire, yet a miraculous silence continued to enfold them as they sailed on unopposed, ghosts upon the building

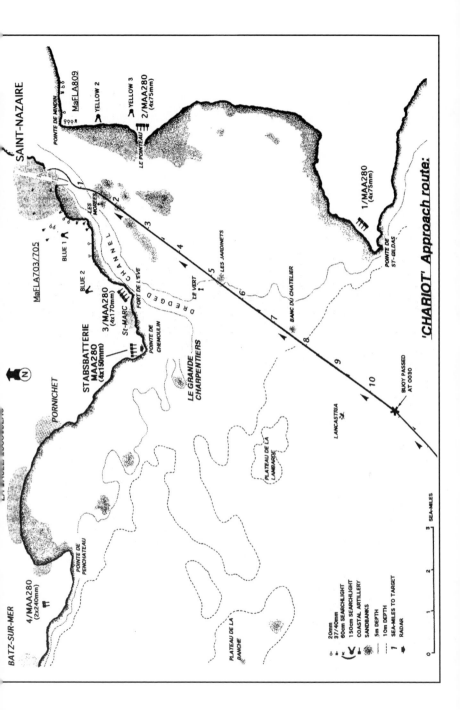

'CHARIOT' Approach route:

SAINT-NAZAIRE

BATZ-SUR-MER

PORNICHET

POINTE DE MINDIN

MaFLA809

YELLOW 2

YELLOW 3

2/MAA280
(4x75mm)

LE POINTEAU

1/MAA280
(4x75mm)

POINTE DE
ST-GILDAS

LES MORÉES

BLUE 1

MaFLA703/705

BLUE 2

3/MAA280
(4x170mm)

St-MARC

FORT DE L'ÈVE

STABSBATTERIE
MAA280
(4x150mm)

POINTE DE
CHEMOULIN

LE VERT

LES JARDINETS

BANC DU CHATELIER

LE GRANDE
CHARPENTIERS

PLATEAU DE LA
LAMBARDE

LANCASTRIA

BUOY PASSED
AT 0030

POINTE DE
PENCHATEAU

PLATEAU DE LA
BANCHE

CHANNEL

DREDGED

N

20mm
37/40mm
60cm SEARCHLIGHT
150cm SEARCHLIGHT
COASTAL ARTILLERY
SANDBANKS
5m DEPTH
10m DEPTH
SEA-MILES TO TARGET
RADAR

SEA-MILES

0   1   2   3

67

HMS *Campbeltown* on her final voyage, trying to look like a German destroyer. DAVID STOGDON

tide.

Eight miles off their port beam, guarding the northern entrance to the estuary, lay the powerful *Batterie de Kermoisan*. Emplaced a little to the east of Batz-sur-Mer, this, the fourth battery of Dieckmann's MAA280, consisted of two elderly 240mm rail-mounted cannon obtained from the French artillery reserve. Dating from the previous conflict, each weighed close to 150 tonnes and had a 360 degree traverse. A similar battery planned for Préfailles, at the western extremity of the opposite estuary shore, was not yet operational, leaving the four 75mm guns of *1/MAA280*, at Pointe St Gildas to take up the slack. Also French in origin these 75s were mounted in the open, their emplacements a mere three miles from Ryder's initial point of entry.

As *Campbeltown* cleared the first shoals and steamed deeper into the estuary, she would pass within a mile and a half of the positions which represented the heart of Dieckmann's defence. Clustered around St-Marc, and including both naval radar and Dieckmann's own headquarters, these consisted of the strategically situated *Stabsbatterie Chémoulin*, and the powerful *Batterie Behncke-West* [*3/MAA280*], which dominated the heights of the nearby Pointe de l'Eve.

The *Stabsbatterie* consisted of four 150mm cannon, of Czech origin, which were emplaced on the cliffs of the Pointe de Chémoulin and concealed under nets. While deadly in themselves these were a much less potent force than the four purpose-designed, quick-firing 170mm naval cannon installed on the site of the old French Fort de l'Eve. Protected from both surface and aerial attack by enormously strong concrete casemates, these were served by some one hundred and fifty men, their ammunition safely stored in a complex of underground galleries. Facing south and west so as to dominate the entrance to the estuary, their one crucial disadvantage in action would be the limitations imposed on their eastward traverse by the very bunkers built to protect them.

Dieckmann's final battery position was that of 2/MAA280 at Le Pointeau, on the estuary shore directly opposite the Fort de l'Eve. A twin of 1/MAA280 at St Gildas, *Batterie le Pointeau* consisted of four of the same captured French 75s, similarly emplaced in the open.

Beyond this point, where the estuary tightened to a choke point little more than a mile wide, surface defence became the responsibility of Mecke's 22.*Marine-Flak-Regiment*, whose *809th Battalion [MaFLA809]*, occupied the eastern shoreline all the way to the Pointe de Mindin. Mecke himself was headquartered not far from Dieckmann, in the Château de St-Marc. His *703rd* and *705th* Battalions secured the defence of the western shoreline, up to and including Saint-Nazaire and the immediate port approaches. Both commanders disposed of medium batteries whose primary function was anti-aircraft defence. None of these would, however, present a threat to the CHARIOT force.

At approximately the same time as *Campbeltown's* groundings, the force sighted, and was sighted by, a small vessel patrolling off the entrance to the Charpentiers channel. Inexplicably, the vessel was not equipped with a radio, and its attempts to use its searchlight to raise interest on shore brought no response. In fact the first of Ryder's ships had penetrated deep inside the estuary before a sighting was made by anyone in a position to do something about it.

By 0100, the ineffective air raid had all but petered out. Mecke had doused his searchlights and ordered his guns to cease firing but, still intrigued by the bombers' strange display, had stopped short of standing his battalions down. As there had been no reports of parachutists, he took the additional precaution of issuing orders that his men pay special attention seaward. It was only at this point that *Korvettenkapitän* Lothar Burhenne, commanding *MaFLA809* from his headquarters in St-Brévin, saw the force approaching and reported the presence of unidentified ships to the office of the Port Commander, *Korvettenkapitän* Ernst Kellermann. Perhaps because Kellermann himself was on leave, Burhenne's report was not taken seriously, at which point he passed it on to Mecke instead, the delay perpetuating the comedy of errors which was allowing the Charioteers to encroach ever deeper into the estuary with every passing minute. Yes, it was dark; and yes, the ships had all been painted a dull mauve to help them blend into the background: but it is still difficult for anyone standing today amidst the still inviolate bunkers of the Fort de l'Eve, to conceive of how so many vessels could pass so close to shore without setting off

Left: The crew of MGB *314*. Bill Savage, who would be awarded a posthumous Victoria Cross for his actions during the raid, is shown without a beard, far right. Above: Motor Gun Boat *314*.

a myriad alarms. No one had seriously expected the British to launch a sea-borne assault on so well defended a target, so far from friendly bases – and therein lay the problem. Only the previous day, Admiral Dönitz, travelling down from his HQ at nearby Kerneval, had visited the port and been assured by the CO of the 7th U-Flotilla, *Korvettenkapitän* Herbert Sohler, that the base was safe from attack. The statement reflected an optimism Dönitz did not share, though he could never have imagined that his adjuration that Sohler be less confident,

MTB 74 at speed.

would be borne out either so quickly, or to the extent where Dönitz himself would be forced to move his U-Boat HQ to Paris, far away from the suddenly vulnerable coastline.

At 0015, a lookout reported the presence of the ships to Dieckmann: and at 0018 the HQ of the Harbour Commander, responding to a query from one of Mecke's staff, confirmed that no friendly ships were expected. Still the precious minutes dragged by, the gunboat passing to starboard of the disused Les Morées light tower, at 0120. This put *Campbeltown* within two miles of the dock caisson, the pressure of expectation almost palpable as her Commando parties and crew waited, second by second, for hell to break loose around them.

Throughout the fleet all guns were trained and ready, the Commandos prepared to add the weight of their own fire to that of the Navy gunners. On the destroyer's foredeck, the Gunner (T), Mr Harold Hargreaves, RN, was in position to control the fire of the 12-pounder, an antiquated weapon with a two-piece projectile. Crouching only a matter of feet behind, Copland realised that the Flak had stopped:

> But I did not feel surprised as it seemed as though the German AA guns were only awaiting the next wave of RAF planes to begin their damage again. On we sailed in that hushed river, no sound save the steady beat of our engines and our own murmured conversation. I had told the No 1 of the gun crew ahead of me to concentrate his fire on enemy searchlights when the action started and all the time I could see the crew ahead of me, dusky movements, alert for the first glimmer of light, but

'The base is safe from attack.'
Korvettenkapitän Herbert Sohler (above)
assured Admiral Dönitz (left).

Typical Fairmile 'B' ML.

The Germans were still unsure about the identity of the fleet of ships heading towards the port. A German gunner lines up on a target.

controlled, knowing that they were not to open fire until the orders were given.

(Major W O Copland, DSO: unpublished narrative)

On board the gunboat Newman, who to Holman's recollection had been 'unconcernedly' smoking his pipe below as the force had entered the estuary, was watching on deck when the scales were finally cast from the defenders' eyes. His record of events describes the way in which:

Suddenly, away astern, two vivid beams of light shot out – a searchlight on each bank of the river swept the water low, and with a sigh of relief it was seen that they had just missed us – the beams joined just aft of the last pair of MLs – against their beams one could see silhouetted the entire force in perfect formation and for the moment, safe. On we went, occasionally testing by Asdic

how far we were off the southern bank. We wanted to hug this
coastline as near as possible. With approximately a quarter of an
hour to go from zero – suddenly on our port side another
searchlight flashed out – and this time bang on the
Campbeltown.

(Lieutenant Colonel A C Newman, VC: unpublished narrative)
The beam emanated from the 150cm searchlight, *'Blau 1'*, situated close
by *Korvettenkapitän* Hans Thiessen's *MaFLA703* HQ, at La Vecquerie.
Mecke having issued the emergency signal 'Landegefahr!', on receipt
of which all units were to prepare to repel an enemy landing, the
sudden appearance of its brilliant beam should have initiated both a
general illumination of the river and an immediate and overwhelming
deluge of fire. However, Ryder's deception plan still had legs, the first
and most important of which belonged to his signals specialist,
Leading Signalman Pike, a rating who had been included in the force
because he could send and receive the Morse code in German.

Even as late as 0123, by which time Ryder's leading elements were
almost within sight of the harbour entrance, the Germans were still
sufficiently unsure of their identity as to challenge the ships by light.
Intelligence having once more worked its magic, Ryder had been
provided with both the morse-names of Schmidt's torpedo-boats and
the recognition pyrotechnics appropriate for that particular time on
that particular day. In an attempt to further confuse the issue, he also
planned to make use of internationally recognized distress signals
when fired upon. In his own words:

When passing Les Morées tower or thereabouts, we were
challenged by a shore station (to port) and Pike replied with one
of our call signs, and without waiting weighed straight in with
"Have urgent signal: two damaged ships in company: request
permission to proceed in without delay". The fact that we were
in actual communication with their own signal station clearly
had a sobering effect. We had not finished this signal when, to
my consternation, we were challenged again, by another signal
station further up near the dockyard. Pike was told to make the
signal "Wait" to the first signal station and then to repeat his
pre-arranged message to the second station.

Although at various moments some sporadic fire was directed
against us, our signalling undoubtedly caused a considerable
degree of hesitation – but as was to be expected, it didn't last
long. These were tense and exciting moments. It does not fall to
everyone's lot to find themselves signalling with the enemy. The
time soon came to play our next card. The International Signal

[for ships being fired upon by their own side]. *This again helped a bit and of course we were getting nearer, so every second mattered. Finally the time came for the Ace of Trumps. This was to be my personal contribution. I fired the Vereys* [sic] *Pistol in the air, hopefully. ...Alas, instead of sailing up into the air for all to see, it dropped miserably into the sea. The fight was on. The signal cartridges obtained in great secrecy were for use from our aircraft firing downwards. No one was to know what we wanted them for. So much for my "ace".*

(Captain R E D Ryder, VC, RN: unpublished narrative)

Ryder's 'bag of tricks' had managed to win a further five precious minutes of grace. On first crossing into the shallows, there had still been eight potentially deadly miles to traverse; yet, unbelievably, the ships had by now already crossed almost seven of these, their presence seemingly enfolded in a miracle of silence. By 0128, however, the enemy's confusion was finally at an end, the belated German acceptance of the fleet as hostile taking the form of a shattering cannonade which burst forth from every gun that would bear. The leading British ships might have been little more than a single mile from their landing sites: but in that instant, every tortured inch of it was transmuted into chaos.

Chapter Six

STEEL TIDE RUNNING

Armed with a Bren gun and stationed amidships on ML 457, 'Tiger' Watson describes the moment when the raiders' bluff was finally called:

All hell was let loose. The air was suddenly full of the deceptively slow-seeming sparkling arcs of the shells, tracer, explosive and incendiary from the quickfiring Bofors guns. They were coming at us at point blank range. Then the heavier coastal guns joined in but I was not conscious of these bigger shells splashing about us. I was too distracted by all this hostile activity from the north bank to see the Campbeltown *lower the German flag and break out the British battle ensign while all our little ships...did the same. But I heard* [Lt] *Tom Collier's klaxon giving the order to his bow and stern Oerlikons to fire, and standing with the Bren gun held at the hip, I directed a stream of tracer at the nearest searchlight.*

(Dr W H Watson, MBE., MC: unpublished narrative)

Still in the van of the formation, the gunboat was closing rapidly on the harbour approaches. Completely exposed on her foredeck, Frank Smith and Bill Savage brought their pom pom into action, the deafening noise of its discharge compelling Sub Lieutenant Worsley to vacate his chosen position at Frank Smith's feet. From their vantage point up on the open bridge, the moment when their world of quiet order suddenly went mad was imprinted forever on the memories of the two commanders, Newman recalling that:

The noise was terrific – tracer of every colour seemed to pour into our fleet – the Campbeltown's *sides seemed to be alive with bursting shells and on the bridge of the gunboat we could watch the stream of tracer coming towards us and it seemed as if one could just duck below it as it passed overhead!*

(Lieutenant Colonel A C Newman, VC: unpublished narrative)

For Ryder, who was painfully aware that their 'diversionary' air-support was nowhere to be seen, it was,

Difficult to describe the full fury of the attack that was let loose on each side. ...In the MGB we were heading close past the bows of a guard ship, probably one of the German flak ships and not above two hundred yards away. This was our target. She opened fire from the top of her bridge with some light automatic weapon, perhaps we were too low for her other guns to bear, anyhow, she only fired one burst. Our Pom Pom instantly scored a direct hit on the gun position and plastered the ship from end to end. This ship with her light camouflage paint and high structure stood out clear in the searchlights and was easily the most conspicuous ship in the river. As we looked back over our shoulders...we were glad to see the enemy shooting at her and hitting her all over the place.

(Captain R E D Ryder, VC, RN: unpublished narrative)

The German vessel, which had been clearly visible on aerial photographs, was *Sperrbrecher 137*, the 996 GRT *Botilla Russ*, a unit of *2.Sperrbrecherflottille*. Armed with one 88mm, and several 20mm, cannon, she had the misfortune to be directly in the path of every ship in the fleet each of which, in turn, would pour fire into her as they passed, leaving her seriously damaged and ablaze.

Some way behind the gunboat and the striking force of ML *160* and ML *270*, *Campbeltown* was also being repeatedly hit as she raced towards the dry dock. Watson, on ML *457*, caught a glimpse of her,

Ploughing along, brilliantly lit up by the accursed searchlights, the British battle ensign streaming out over her

HMS *Campbeltown* showing her 12-pounder gun and modifications to the bridge superstructure. In view is the screen at the base of the bridge behind which 'Major Bill' took station. LISLE RYDER

stern...her sides alive with the flashes of the shells which were hitting her continuously. It was a sight that I shall never forget.

(Dr W H Watson, MBE., MC: unpublished narrative)

Seemingly trapped within a vortex of fire, *Campbeltown* was certainly taking a beating. However, as she had already slipped past the outer coastal batteries unseen, and as their limited traverse no longer allowed the Fort de l'Eve guns to bear, the old destroyer was now being peppered with shells the majority of which lacked the weight to inflict any terminal damage. To the watching 'Major Bill' Copland,

it seemed as though every gun on earth had opened fire on us. In immediate reply, our Oerlikon guns aft opened up with their deadly crackle and I yelled to the gun crew and mortar crews ahead to "Let her go". Almost before I had finished shouting, the first rounds had gone off from the 12- pounder and our mortars. Before the next round was fired by them, I was deafened and thrown about by a terrific explosion which appeared to come almost from my feet. The smoke cleared and looking ahead I saw the mortars and crews intact but the 12-pounder crew had vanished and, directly in front of me yawned a gaping, smoking hole and about two thirds the width of the deck. I thought about two things – "God, what rotten luck" and "Probably 4 inch and marvellous shooting". How we got through the next thirteen minutes with anyone left alive, will always pass my understanding.

(Major W O Copland, DSO: unpublished narrative)

Copland attributed the hit to coastal artillery, while Beattie blamed a 'large Thermite bomb' for the damage. Private Bill Holland, who was crewing the starboard mortar when the missile struck, believes this was when Lieutenant Johnny Proctor sustained the wound which would ultimately cost him his leg.

Hugging the deck behind *Campbeltown's* starboard inner armoured screen, Lieutenant Stuart Chant, his ears assailed by constant explosions and the clanging of red-hot splinters slamming into steel, saw one of the Oerlikon gunners on the midships platform just above collapse in his sling as he was hit. His shouted warning that everyone should keep their heads down presaged an explosion nearby which, in peppering Chant with shrapnel, sounded for all the world, 'like the noise of someone banging a steel door with a sledgehammer'. The fire from Mecke's cannon was particularly telling at such close range, the German missiles only having to strike hull or superstructure to have a deadly effect. Lying on deck with the others, Lieutenant Bill Etches describes being hit, by fire coming from the south bank of the estuary, after the ship had been illuminated by searchlights. This was from 20 or 30mm light anti-aircraft weapons firing in bursts of five or six rounds at a range of not much above 1000m initially... . These light AA cannon shells were dusting and spraying the decks...with splinters, several of which I collected in both legs, in my right buttock and right arm, as a result of which I was in considerable pain and fairly immobile...

(Colonel W W Etches, OBE.,MC: letter to author, 10 August 1994)
Having judged it prudent to vacate *Campbeltown's* open signal platform, Beattie was now conning the ship from the shelter of her armoured bridge. Amongst those sharing the compartment with him

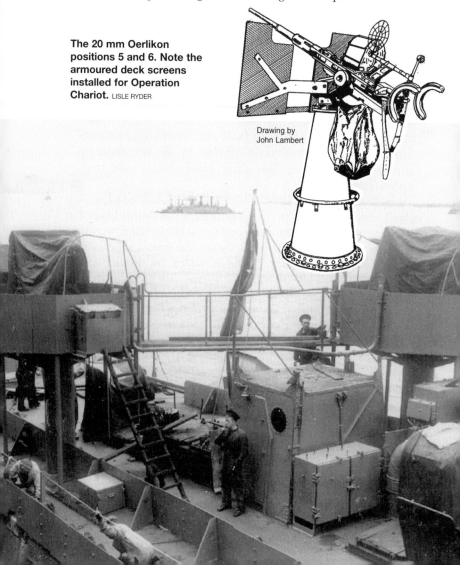

The 20 mm Oerlikon positions 5 and 6. Note the armoured deck screens installed for Operation Chariot. LISLE RYDER

Drawing by
John Lambert

were Tibbits, fulfilling the role of Navigating Officer, and Montgomery. With the view forward restricted to a slim aperture in the protective plating, the dimly-lit space was soon reverberating to missile strikes whose impact caused chips and splinters to fly from interior surfaces. Beattie it was who had given the signal to open fire: however, as his narrative confirms, the ship had already been hit a number of times prior to the hoisting of the British battle ensign:

> *The first serious hit entered the ship's office, below the bridge structure, at about 0119. It was about 4" calibre and put the LP* [Low Pressure] *generator out of action and wounded SPO* [Stoker Petty Officer] *Pitt, who was in charge of the forecastle fire party. The ship was also hit by machine gun bullets in the bridge and funnels. This was before* Campbeltown *opened fire.*
> (Lieutenant Commander S H Beattie, VC, RN: 'Narrative of HMS
> *Campbeltown* at St Nazaire, 28 March, 1942')

The destroyer's steel plating offered considerably better protection than was to be found on board the MLs: however, under the full weight of the enemy barrage, those within were still at risk from penetrating shot and shell. The demolition parties of Brett and Purdon were stationed in the wardroom, and Purdon vividly recalls the 'hammering and explosions' of missiles striking the hull, and how, 'A shell, glowing red, passed through...as we sat there, but continued out without exploding.' Deep within the bowels of the ship, and out of sight of the drama unfolding in the world beyond, the engineers, artificers and stokers were particularly at risk, Beattie remarking on how, 'in the engine-room a hail of German fire could be heard striking the ship, and bullets were ricochetting about in the engine-rooms and boiler-rooms'. Up on deck, those of the gunners and crew who were especially exposed to enemy fire, had begun to suffer casualties at an early stage and were being tended by the Saskatchewan-born Surgeon Lieutenant Winthrope, RCNVR. These were brought together in the shelter of the cramped well-deck, where they would later prove an obstacle to Copland's parties attempting to disembark.

The large missile which had exploded forward had broken through the foredeck and started a fire in the Chief Petty Officers' mess, directly above the ship's all-important demolition charge. SPO Pitt having already been incapacitated, the forward fire control party was taken over by Leading Stoker Baxter, RN, whose men succeeded in bringing the blaze under control.

Beattie having rung down for 200 revolutions, *Campbeltown* was steaming through the smoke and spray at eighteen and a half knots for what appeared to be the lighthouse at the eastern end of the Old Mole. At this point a combination of poor visibility and blinding searchlights almost put paid to the whole affair, for only at the very last minute did Beattie realise that the ship was actually steering straight for the mouth of the Avant Port. His narrative continues

it was eventually seen that Campbeltown *was approaching the Avant Port, and the wheel was put hard a starboard at 0129 and course altered to 055. As the ship was swinging, the lighthouse on the Old Mole was lit by a sweeping German searchlight for a second or two, and this gave the necessary direction to steer. The ship passed within about half a cable of the Old Mole and course was altered to 350 to take her up to the lock. By the time the ship reached the Old Mole the coxswain* [CPO Wellsted] *had been wounded and had to relinquish the wheel to the telegraphman who was also, I think, wounded, and was trying to steer while lying on the deck. Lieutenant Tibbits then took over the wheel, altered round the Old Mole and steered the ship to the lock.*

(Lieutenant Commander S H Beattie, VC, RN: 'Narrative of HMS *Campbeltown* at St Nazaire, 28 March, 1942')

Out in front of the destroyer, the gunboat and the two torpedo-armed supporting launches – Lieutenant Irwin's ML *270* on the port side and Lieutenant Tom Boyd's ML *160* to starboard – had all reached the harbour in one piece. All three were manoeuvring in the fairway south and east of the 'Normandie' dock, MGB *314* to keep Ryder and Newman in visual contact with *Campbeltown* and the remaining ships of the fleet; ML *160* and ML *270* to suppress enemy searchlights and gun defences in the immediate vicinity of Beattie's line of approach.

Clustered as they were around and astern of *Campbeltown*, the story of the troop-carrying MLs was quickly tinged with tragedy. With so much heavy fire being directed against the one large ship, those in her general area suffered particularly, Billie Stephens' ML192 being amongst the first to succumb. Leading the starboard column, *192* carried an assault team made up of Captain Micky Burn, Lieutenant Tom Peyton, and twelve other ranks from their tightly-bonded 6 Troop: 2 Commando. In light of the fate awaiting them, Micky's memory of how the ship had been as she entered the estuary, every man at his station, is particularly poignant, his text describing how:

I went round my group, standing to by the two 20mm crew-manned guns or lying down behind Brens, or simply with grenades and Tommy-gun, and wished each man luck. Tom Peyton was in command of the soldiers aft. I stayed forward of Billie Stephens [Lieutenant Commander RNVR] *who was on the bridge and commanded all the MLs. I had with me Harrison*

[Lance Sergeant Maurice, known as "Boy"] *and one or two others. Right forward, sunk into his hatch, Willie Bell* [Fusilier William "Dingle"] *had become a round face and a steel helmet. By one o'clock we could smell the countryside and see outlines of houses and hedgerows on both banks. By twenty minutes past one, with a mile and three-quarters to go, a searchlight went on astern, swept on towards our last craft – and went out. We could still believe ourselves to be undetected.*

(Michael Burn, MC., *Turned Towards the Sun*: pp135-6)

Trailing *Campbeltown* on the destroyer's starboard quarter, Micky's small and perfect universe was all too soon shattered by a succession of shells which struck the ML's port side. On fire and with her engines

Michael Burn, MC. OC 6 Troop, 2 Commando. On ML *192*.
MICHAEL BURN

and steering knocked out, *192* slewed to port, crossed the bow of ML*447*, and, completely out of control, crashed into the south face of the Old Mole between gun position 63 and searchlight LS21. In registering the shock and confusion of the sudden transformation, Micky's account recalls how he,

> *was aware of buildings, a wall towering up, and heard Billie Stephens shout, "Jump! Now's your chance!"*
>
> *"Why?" I thought. "What for? We haven't landed."*
>
> *I told Harrison to follow me, went to the starboard rail and looked aft. The ship was on fire, sheering rapidly away from a stone wall. I jumped, loaded with grenades, swam a few strokes and thought I was going to drown.* [Lance Corporal] *Arthur Young had already jumped and landed on steps in the wall. He had been wounded in the foot, but sitting there he managed to reach an arm far enough to lug me on to them. The ML bumped away. Firing was going on all round, but, sheltered by the wall, we saw little of it. Searchlights illumined the river. A strong high tide swept beneath our feet, carrying past us, out of reach, a body in British uniform, face down. I saw that it was Tom Peyton.*
>
> (Michael Burn, MC., *Turned Towards the Sun* pp 136-7)

Lieutenant Commander S H Beattie.

'Boy'Harrison had also been killed: indeed, of the fourteen Commandos of 6 Troop, only six were to survive the night, these including Micky whose adventures, though he didn't know it yet, were only just beginning. Finally cleared of the living, most of whom evacuated onto the nearby Quai René Kerviler, ML*192*, blazing furiously, drifted southwards with the tide.

With Lieutenant Platt's ML*447* at the head of the port column, sweeping round the Mole to attempt a landing at its north-side slipway, *Campbeltown* positively raced through the final metres of her impossible journey. With the Mole lighthouse fast disappearing behind her port quarter, Beattie recalls how,

> *A slight check was felt as the ship went through the torpedo net but she*

Southern face of the Old Mole, showing the steps which proved the salvation of Captain Micky Burn and other survivors of ML*192*.

was not thrown off her course. As she parted the net the wheel was ordered Port 20, as the lock could then be plainly seen and the ship was not going quite straight for the middle. It was also desirable to throw the stern slightly to Starboard to prevent from blocking the way to the Old Entrance.

(Lieutenant Commander S H Beattie, VC.,RN: 'Narrative of HMS *Campbeltown* at St Nazaire, 28 March, 1942')

Out in the open, forward of the bridge, Copland describes the ship as having become, by this stage, 'A floating collander'. The 12-pounder gun-crew having been pulled back out of danger following the big explosion on the fo'c's'le, he had a virtually uninterrupted view ahead, and could see,

the Dock-Gate – black against the concrete of the dock walls, nearer and nearer it came and blacker and blacker it appeared. With hardly a tremor we cut through the submarine boom – 18 knots and only 100 yards to go – the time 1.32 am. We hung on like grim death to any projection, expecting a terrific shock and then – impact! A feeling as though one had applied super-powerful brakes to a very small car and – STOP! The debris from the shock of our own impact fell all about our bows, sparks, dirt and planks seemed to be flying everywhere and from our bows poured a dense white smoke cloud.

(Major W O Copland, DSO: unpublished narrative)

The gunboat, having sheered off to starboard to clear *Campbeltown's* route to the gate, was momentarily lost to the searchlights and had a grandstand view of the destroyer grinding over the solid, black face of the caisson. Fire was still pouring into her, and in spite of having struck, her Oerlikons continued to douse nearby enemy positions with streaking fronds of tracer. Almost incredibly, after all the long weeks of planning, training and petty vexations, a combination of expert navigation, adroit ship handling and – it would have to be said – good fortune, had brought their floating bomb precisely onto target.

Her own, rather more modest, odyssey still very far from complete, there was only a moment for those on board the MGB to marvel at Beattie's seamanship before it was time to return to the heart of the action. She had in the interim been taking her own share of hits, her commander, Lieutenant Dunstan Curtis reporting that:

> *Within ten minutes of the beginning of the action, the starboard .5 turret in MGB 314 received 4 direct hits from Oerlikon shells. As a result the feed pipes of the power system were severed in four or five places, and the turret was put out of action. Furthermore the whole power system was emptied of fluid in a very short time; a process which was accelerated by further leaks, which started as a result of the port .5 turret being hit in its turn and put out of action.*
>
> *Fortunately the pom pom in 314 was hand operated: had it been power operated it would also have been immobilized.*

(Lieutenant D M C Curtis, DSC., RNVR. Action report)

The after gun having become unserviceable earlier in the day, the firepower of this, the most heavily armed of the 'little ships', was therefore substantially reduced early on, the loss exacerbated by the earlier decision to include no others of her kind in the fleet.

With *Campbeltown* embedded in the caisson, the battle had resolved itself into two entirely separate struggles: that of her own Commandos; and that of the columns of MLs, now fracturing into a confusion of boats, some aflame, some disabled, which seemed to stretch from one side of the river to the other. Ryder, whose first responsibility was to assist the ships in their struggle to reach the landing places, found it;

> *difficult to see clearly what was happening to all our craft at this stage owing to the glare of searchlights and the confusion of flying tracer bullets.*

Relatively close at hand it could be seen that Boyd's ML160, having completed her preparatory bombardment of the coastline to starboard of *Campbeltown*, had sped up the river in search of new targets. However, Irwin's ML270 was, at least for the moment, nowhere to be seen.

German searchlight with crew.

20 mm Flak crew.

Further off, the flaming wreck of Stephens' ML192 was clearly visible, drifting south of the Mole. The crew of the *Sperrbrecher* had obviously recovered their courage and composure, as her guns were again engaging the milling MLs. Some shape, or shapes, could be seen approaching the Old Entrance, as per orders: but as for the rest, organization and intent had clearly fallen foul of defences from whose killing power their structure and armament offered little protection.

It was at this critical point that the difficulties naturally inherent in splitting command, came to the fore. According to Ryder's recollection of events, 'By this time we had circled round and as Colonel Newman was anxious to get ashore, we nosed our way in.' In fact Ryder, clearly troubled by the fate of the MLs and the effect of the *Sperrbrecher's* renewed barrage, wanted to make assisting them his first priority, Newman recalling that, on circling,

> *Our first sight was a German Flak Ship moored just off the Old Mole belching forth fire. Ryder was for giving orders to find an ML fitted with torpedoes to deal with her immediately, but I was too anxious to be put shore. ...A hasty argument and he altered course to land us first in the Old Entrance.*

(Lieutenant Colonel A C Newman, VC: unpublished narrative)
The two ambitions – of Ryder to give much needed help to his ships, and of Newman to take immediate control of his men ashore – were, of course, mutually exclusive. Someone had to lose, and that someone was Ryder, for, having nosed into the deep socket that was the Old Entrance, he would remain out of sight, and control, of his ships until far too late to effect any kind of recovery.

Chapter Seven

ALL SMOKE: NO MIRRORS

As MGB*314* made for shore, the distant flames as yet only hinted at the fate in store for wooden boats sent to do the job of armoured ships. Constructed from plywood frames to which were attached a skin of mahogany planking, the MLs offered negligable protection from even the lightest of projectiles. Powered by two 600hp Hall-Scott 'Defender' engines, they were fuelled by petrol, the normal load of 2,200 gallons supplemented by self-sealing deck-tanks. In action they would prove to be little better than fire traps.

Lieutenant Curtis, commander of MGB *314*. MRS P. CURTIS

The plan of attack had called for both columns of troop-carrying MLs to enter the port tipped with the steel of assault parties. In the case of the port formation, heading for the Old Mole, this ambition had already been fatally weakened by the transfer of Hodgson's troops to the trailing ML*446* and in the case of the starboard formation it had been completely nullified by Stephens' sudden swerve out of line, ML*192's* abrupt departure promoting Lieutenant Ted Burt's ill-equipped ML*262* to lead boat in the mad dash to reach the shelter of the Old Entrance.

Steaming through a maelstrom of tracer and blinding searchlights, Burt took immediate action to avoid becoming the next victim of the same, deadly battery. Already at a disadvantage because his forward Oerlikon kept jamming, he had only five 'fighting' troops on board, these consisting of Lieutenant Dick Morgan and the small team with which he was to 'protect' Lieutenant Mark Woodcock's Demolition party 2A. A combination of impossible visibility, allied to his own evasive manoeuvrings and Beattie's sudden turn to starboard, led the boat to plough on past the 'Normandie' dock. In his action report, Burt

89

describes how he had,

> lost touch with the **Campbeltown** *and had also missed the Old Entrance. I afterwards found that Lieutenant Commander Beattie had had to alter course to Starboard in order to avoid the Old Mole, thus making his final alteration of course to the Lock Gate more drastic than originally intended, and also that I had taken my bearings from the line of gantrys [sic] on the Starboard side of the Dry Dock instead of those on the port side. I then reduced speed to eight knots and felt my way close inshore, having to... avoid a dredger at anchor off the Building Slip... .*

(Lieutenant E A Burt, DSC, RNVR. Action report)
The building slip referred to was occupied by the unfinished aircraft carrier, *Joffre*. On turning short round with the intention of making his way back to the landing site, Burt found that he was not alone in having missed the turn for, similarly confused by the rapid collapse of their orderly formation, Lieutenant Eric Beart had followed him up-river. Beart's ML267 carried RSM Alan Moss, his ten-man reserve and the special thirty-five-star rockets whose firing was to announce the start of the withdrawal. The two boats came together and Beart called out, 'Where the hell are we?' in response to which entreaty Burt, 'gave

him his position over the loud hailer, set my course at approximately 260 degrees and increased speed to twelve knots.'

Having begun the approach with six troop-carrying MLs, the starboard column had now lost three in rapid succession – with one destroyed and two out of position upstream. The fourth in line, Lieutenant Bill Tillie's ML268, had only just made its turn towards the Old Entrance when it was set ablaze by enemy fire, blowing up shortly thereafter. This boat had carried a further seven men of Moss's reserve, the five-man demolition team of Lieutenant Harry Pennington, and a five-man protection squad commanded by Second Lieutenant Morgan Jenkins. Of the seventeen Commandos all but two were lost: and of their naval brothers, Tillie was fortunate to be counted amongst the seven out of fifteen who survived the pitiless conflagration. Pennington was amongst the many for

Second Lieutenant Morgan Jenkins. PETER COPLAND

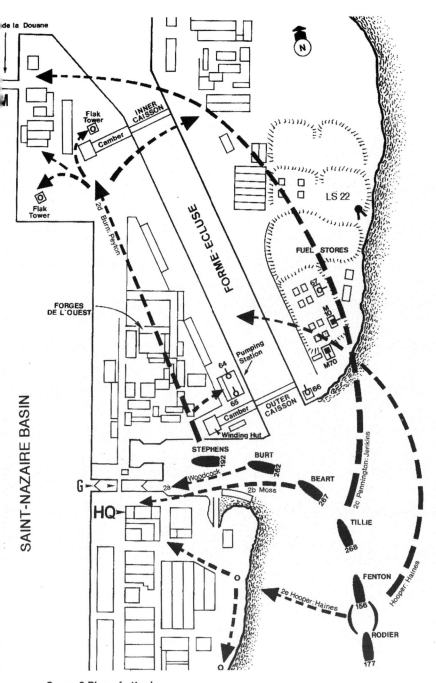

Group 2 Plan of attack

TSM George Haines, Hythe, 1940.
MRS P. HAINES

whom the night would bring fulfilment of the conviction that they would not return. The loss of Jenkins, Micky Burn's paragon of 'celtic charm', along with his four companions, made grimmer still the statistic that was already biting deep into the heart of 6 Troop.

The remaining two boats of the starboard column were torpedo-armed MLs from the 7th Flotilla. Together they carried the twenty-eight men of special task party 2E who, upon landing were to investigate suspected gun positions close to the shore between the Mole and Old Entrance, silence any ships in the dry dock, and then come into HQ reserve. Lieutenant Leslie Fenton's ML156 carried Captain Dickie Hooper, 4 Troop, 2 Commando, together with TSM Tom Sherman and twelve other ranks: Lieutenant Mark Rodier's ML177, at the tail of the line, carried TSM George Haines along with Hooper's remaining tranche of thirteen assault commandos.

Arriving on the scene when the German gunners were really beginning to hit back, Fenton's boat had already been struck a number of times when a burst of cannon shells ripped through the bridge, wounding Fenton and Hooper and spraying TSM Sherman with shrapnel. Amidst the smoke and spray, several boats seemed to be heavily on fire: then another ML, probably Tillie's, blew up ahead. At this point the withdrawal pyrotechnics were mistakenly identified and Fenton, close to collapse and believing that a successful landing was now no longer possible, relinquished control to his Number One, Sub Lieutenant Machin, with instructions to follow other boats out.

Caught in the middle of a vicious crossfire and targeted by the seemingly revitalized *Sperrbrecher*, Machin's report describes how,

> *Having given orders to make smoke, our steering went and I reduced speed in order to try and torpedo a flak ship which was doing us most damage. Instantly, our engines went out of action. I gave orders for the hand-steering to be manned and started to go aft to supervise, but as I got aft of the funnel, I was hit. I then*

made my way to the engine-room to see if we had any chance of starting them and found they had got the starboard engine going.

(Sub Lieutenant N G Machin, DSC., RNVR. Action report)

Fenton having by this time recovered consciousness, he, Hooper and Machin agreed that with the boat in such bad shape and their one remaining engine having to be run full ahead to prevent it from stopping, there was now no alternative but to continue their withdrawal under cover of smoke.

The manoeuvring and subsequent crippling of ML156 had brought Rodier's ML177 up on her port side. Rodier, convinced he would not survive contact with the enemy, had made sure Sub Lieutenant Frank Arkle, his Number One, knew the exact location of all his personal effects. Yet here he was, right at the heart of the action, surrounded by flame, smoke and the dreadful cacophany of battle, his boat, crew and Commando passengers as yet free from the wounds to structure and flesh which were scarring so many others within the fleet.

Running parallel with the shoreline north of the Mole, Rodier slightly overran the turning point before dipping beneath the destroyer's stern to become the first ML to make it into the Old Entrance. Coming alongside the anchorage's southern face he was able to put his Commandos directly onto the quayside. Forming up 'Indian' style, and led by TSM Haines, these melted speedily into the deep shadow of nearby structures.

ML177 had been one of the 'shapes' observed just moments before by Ryder, who was now fast approaching in the gunboat. On coming alongside the timber jetty immediately astern of Rodier, Newman, impatient to be ashore with his boys, exchanged a brief handshake with Ryder before leading his party over the side – onto French soil at

last. His own recollection is that:

> *Murdoch and Kelly* [Private soldiers acting as Newman's bodyguard] *with their Tommy Guns, closely followed by Stan and I with Sergeant Steele and the wireless set just behind, Terry, Walker and Harrington bringing up the rear, was the order in which we proceeded up the road towards my selected headquarters. There was no sign of any of our other troops, but I fully expected RSM Moss and the Reserve had safely settled themselves in... .*

(Lieutenant Colonel A C Newman, VC: unpublished narrative)
The building selected by Newman was the Hôtel des Ponts et Chaussées, a large structure running parallel with the quayside, but rather closer to the lock gates and bridge. Upon arrival, he would indeed find it occupied – though not by anyone as friendly or welcoming as Moss.

With the HQ party swallowed up by the night, Ryder switched his priorities to *Campbeltown*, the source of so much noise and commotion just outside the anchorage. Bringing the gunboat alongside ML177, he first ordered Rodier to take off as many of *Campbeltown's* crew as he could before making a dash for home; then he instructed Curtis to bring MGB314 around and put him ashore on the northern quayside.

While Ryder was taking personal control in the Old Entrance, Micky Burn was wending his solitary way towards his party's target area, up by Bridge 'M'. Arthur Young having hauled him from the water onto the steps at the south eastern tip of the Mole, Micky's one thought, in spite of everything, had been that he 'must get on,' his account reflecting the conflicting emotions engendered by a combination of shock and the deeply ingrained dictates of training and duty:

> *I scrambled up the steps on to the jetty. A German soldier was lying there. I found myself – the phrase describes someone I had not met before and never wish to meet again – bashing and bashing away at his head with the butt of my Colt revolver* [sic]*. Then I got up to go on. Instead of the neat planned come-alongside at the Old Entrance, I had been hurled on to the Old Mole... This meant* [a] *quarter of a mile more of dockyard to cross to my group's objective at the northern end. They were objectives still, though already no longer for a cohering group. Arthur Young could not walk and would have to stay where he was until re-embarkation. If the others had swum or jumped ashore further down-river, they had individually memorised the objectives and the lay-out of streets and buildings. It was night, we had rehearsed this kind of thing at Ayr and many other places; night had become our*

element, as groups, or if necessary, as now, alone.

North for me meant right-handed, away from the Mole. Beyond should be open space..., beyond that, railway trucks, houses, workshops, cover. There they were. Moonlight, or searchlights, or gunfire, revealed them fitfully. In my immediate way was a gun emplacement with two Germans on top. I doubled across the open space. They had seen me. They must fire. They could not miss. I felt a sharp stab in the inside of my left thigh, another in my right arm, a third in my back. The wounds were to heal in a few days. I was very fit; for small injuries, self-healing.

(Michael Burn, MC: *Turned Towards the Sun* p137)

The Mole was four hundred metres due south of Ryder's position, so Micky's 'quarter mile', given twists and turns, was in reality much closer to a dark and infinitely hostile kilometre. He would struggle on alone, leaving on and around the Mole two groups of survivors. Stranded on the Quai René Kerviler, close to its base, the main group included both Stephens and his Number One, Sub Lieutenant Haighton: while at its very tip a smaller party, led by Sub Lieutenant Collinson, had clambered up the steps and taken shelter within the lighthouse.

During the period of ML192's evacuation, the troop-carrying MLs of the port column had begun their own ill-fated attempts to subdue the Mole defences. Jutting some 125m into the fairway, the height of this

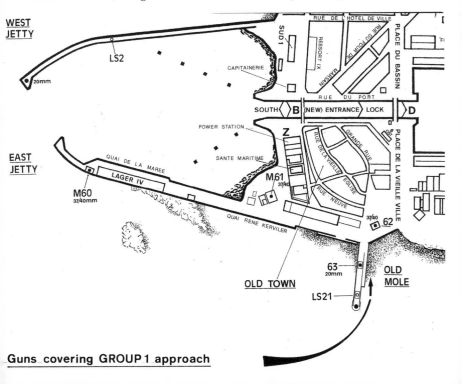

Guns covering GROUP 1 approach

sustantial structure allowed the defenders to pitch grenades down onto the MLs' decks, while requiring the Commandos and naval gunners to shoot upwards at an angle which lessened the effect of much of their own fire. Surrounded at its base by sand and rocks the Mole's upper surface could be accessed only by the steep, narrow steps either side of the lighthouse, or by the wide slipway which ran along much of its northern face. It was for this latter feature, whose gentle incline was supposed to permit assault in force, that six MLs

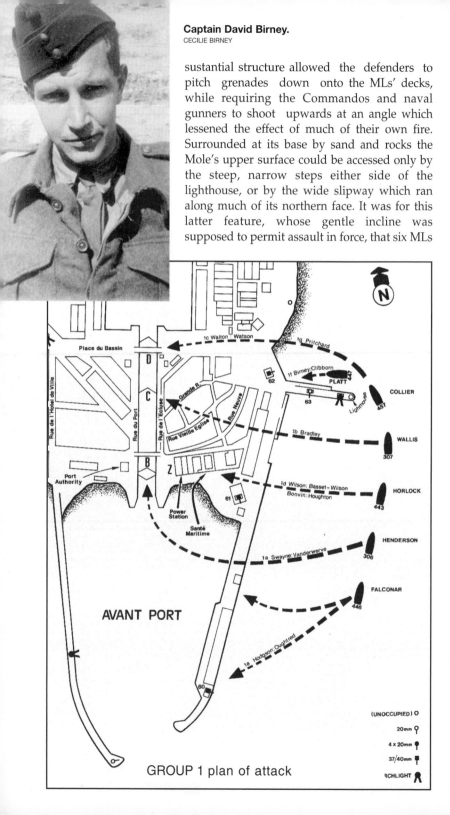

GROUP 1 plan of attack

1. Top: German destroyer *Köln*.

2. Centre: USS *Buchanan* before the refit.

3. Bottom: HMS *Campbeltown* following her conversion to resemble a twin-funnelled German destroyer. It was hoped that the ruse would cause Saint-Nazaire's gunners to hesitate and thereby delay the inevitable fierce defensive fire from the port's guns.

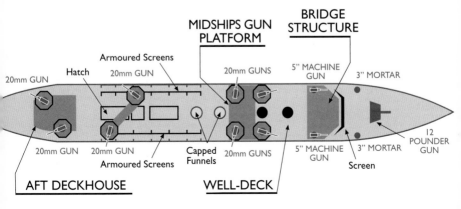

MIDSHIPS GUN PLATFORM

BRIDGE STRUCTURE

Armoured Screens

20mm GUN

Hatch

20mm GUN

20mm GUNS

5" MACHINE GUN

3" MORTAR

20mm GUN

20mm GUN

20mm GUN

Capped Funnels

20mm GUNS

Armoured Screens

5" MACHINE GUN

3" MORTAR

Screen

12 POUNDER GUN

AFT DECKHOUSE

WELL-DECK

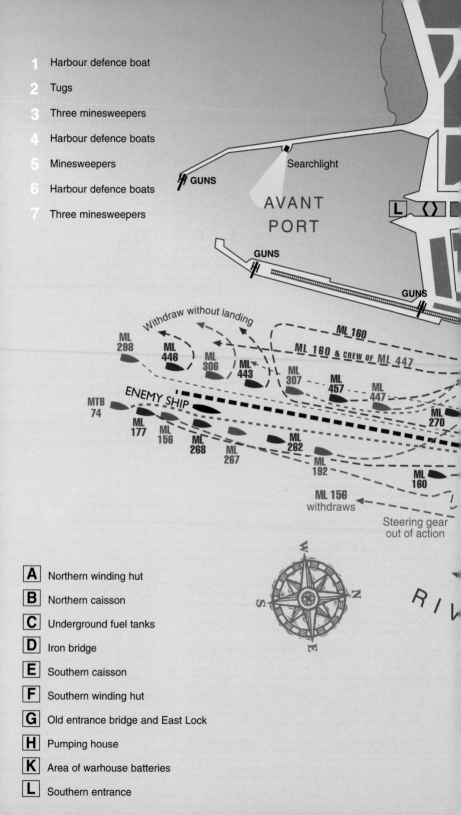

1 Harbour defence boat

2 Tugs

3 Three minesweepers

4 Harbour defence boats

5 Minesweepers

6 Harbour defence boats

7 Three minesweepers

GUNS

Searchlight

AVANT
PORT

L ⟨⟩

GUNS

GUNS

Withdraw without landing

ML 160

ML 298

ML 446

ML 306

ML 443

ML 160 & CREW OF ML 447

ML 307

ML 457

ML 447

MTB 74

ENEMY SHIP

ML 270

ML 177

ML 156

ML 268

ML 267

ML 262

ML 192

ML 160

ML 156
withdraws

Steering gear
out of action

RIV

A Northern winding hut

B Northern caisson

C Underground fuel tanks

D Iron bridge

E Southern caisson

F Southern winding hut

G Old entrance bridge and East Lock

H Pumping house

K Area of warhouse batteries

L Southern entrance

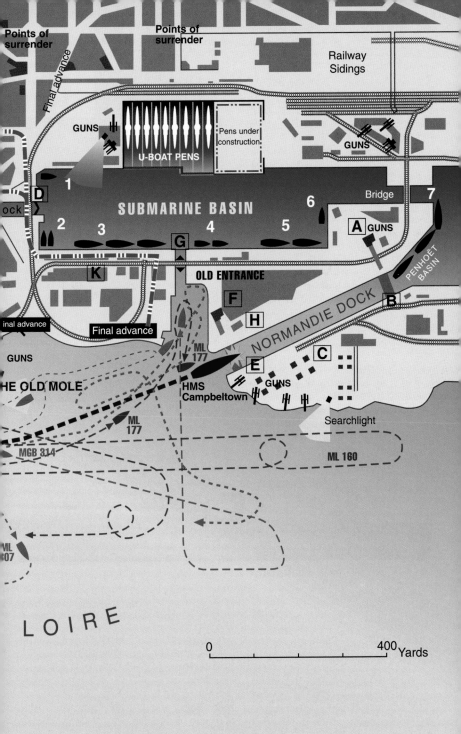

Points of surrender

Points of surrender

Final advance

Railway Sidings

GUNS

U-BOAT PENS

Pens under construction

GUNS

1

D

ock

SUBMARINE BASIN

6

Bridge

7

2

3

4

5

A GUNS

K

G

OLD ENTRANCE

F

B

PENHOËT BASIN

inal advance

Final advance

H

NORMANDIE DOCK

GUNS

E

C

ML 177

THE OLD MOLE

HMS Campbeltown

GUNS

Searchlight

ML 177

MGB 314

ML 160

ML 307

LOIRE

0   400 Yards

HMS *Campbeltown* surges ahead, through a storm of enemy fire.

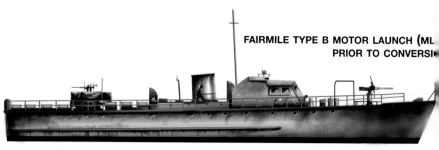

FAIRMILE TYPE B MOTOR LAUNCH (ML
PRIOR TO CONVERSI

Illustration by Jon Wilkinson.

MOTOR GUN BOAT (MGB) 3

VICKERS
2 POUNDER
POM POM

VICKERS
MACHINE
GUNS

ROLLS ROYCE
2 POUNDER

Illustration by Jon Wilkinson.

were now making, their perilous approach requiring them to survive the close-range fire of a succession of enemy guns positioned both along the quaysides to port, and on the Mole itself.

On the East Jetty, gun position M60 stood immediately next to building Lager 1V. At its base, position 61 was a 40mm cannon mounted on top of a powerful bunker. Position 62 covered the base of the Mole, while position 63 was a 20mm cannon sited on top of a two-storey bunker directly above the target slipway. This bunker's twin, carrying searchlight LS21, was further along, closer to the lighthouse and steps.

First to run this gauntlet was Lieutenant Platt's ML447, carrying Captain David Birney and the thirteen men of the only remaining assault Party. Their vital task was to subdue the

Lieutenant Graham Baker. GINA BAKER LAMB

Mole defences and form a bridgehead to protect the structure so it could be used for the final re-embarkation. The building housing gun position 62 was, when cleared, to be used as an aid post by the two Commando doctors and their orderlies.

Running north past the blazing ML192, ML447 turned to port and made for the slipway. Having been one of the foremost boats, she had already suffered numerous hits and casualties, many of Birney's troops having been killed or wounded even before the turn was made. The wheelhouse was reported by Platt as 'riddled with 40mm shell'. The forward Oerlikon had been knocked out and its controlling officer, Lieutenant Chambers, killed at his station. With the after Oerlikon also out of action, the boat was to all intents and purposes defenceless; yet Platt continued to push for the slipway, only to run aground in the steeply shelving water. Lieutenant Graham Baker, a young Canadian officer whose very first command awaited his safe return, prepared, in Platt's words, 'to take a bow rope ashore in the face of intense and constant enemy fire of heavy calibre'. Tragically, while attempting this, he appears to have been hit and lost overboard, for Platt could find no trace of him later, during his thorough inspection of the crippled boat prior to its being abandoned.

Already under damaging cannon attack, 447 was now close enough to the Mole for enemy troops to toss grenades onto her deck from behind the shelter of its low, crowning walls. With a landing at the slipway clearly out of the question, he decided instead to go astern and attempt to bring the boat alongside the steps which led up to the lighthouse. Having succeeded in pulling himself away from the shoal, he had no sooner rung down for 'full-ahead' than the engine-room was set ablaze by a direct hit which knocked out both Hall-Scotts. Dead in the water and still with her bow to the shore, the heavily damaged ML drifted with the tide which, by carrying her stern-first out into the fairway, encouraged those on board the rapidly closing ML457 to assume she was withdrawing after having successfully landed Birney and his men. In fact, with so many casualties and so much petrol still on board, Platt's sole priority was to save what he could of his Commandos and crew. As the wounded were put onto a Carley Float, the handful of Commandos who were still fit enough to swim, set out for the shore. A futile attempt was made to warn the 457 off, after which the Mole, inviolate still, became the concern of others.

Lieutenant Tom Collier's ML457 carried three five-man teams: Captain Bill Pritchard's demolition control party; Lieutenant Philip Walton's team for the destruction of Bridge 'D'; and Second Lieutenant Bill 'Tiger' Watson's protection party. Having been firing hard at searchlight positions on shore, Watson recalls how, during the approach to the Mole:

> We passed by the German ...Sperrbrecher. *She seemed to be listing, with great holes visible in her hull. There was also a small fire...and we were close enough to hear hoarse screams from her interior. I gave a couple of short bursts to the upper deck in case some ill-wisher up there fired down on us. Then we were past and heading for our landing at the Old Mole. I put down the Bren to prepare to land.*
>
> *As we made our approach I saw some German coalscuttle helmets bobbing along the lurid skyline. I quickly reached for the Bren that was leaning against the funnel. I could not miss at that distance. I dropped it quicker than I picked it up as I had seized it by its red-hot barrel. Having retrieved it I now saw that the owners of the coalscuttle helmets were running along the Mole towards the town in a ragged single file with their hands raised. They were obviously surrendering to one of the assault parties.*
>
> *This conclusion was reinforced by the ML which was apparently reversing off from the slipway. I only had time to be aware of the awful screams from another ML which was burning furiously to starboard when we bumped gently against the slipway. Tom Collier had brought us in beautifully.*
>
> *As the landing party lurched to its feet, I was annoyed to find that [Sub Lieutenant] Hampshire and the forward Oerlikon gun crew had not unshipped the ship's rail section which they should now have done in order to enable the heavily*

*laden demolition team to clamber ashore more easily. Then I
realised that Hampshire and his men were lying round their gun
either dead or wounded. But there was no time to lose getting the
rail down ourselves. My party followed me over the rail leaving
the demolition team to follow in its own time.*

(Dr W H Watson, MBE., MC; unpublished narrative)

Running up the slipway directly beneath bunker 63, Watson's small
party should have been at the mercy of the enemy. But the whole
structure was eerily quiet, the inexplicable absence of grenades or
small-arms fire only serving to reinforce the belief that it had already
been cleared by parties which must have gone on ahead. A ladder
leaned against the gun position. 'Tiger' employed it to climb up and
fire a couple of Tommy-gun bursts into the apparently empty interior.
Regrettably, with Pritchard loudly registering his disapproval of
'Tiger's' apparent time-wasting and no sign whatever of the enemy, no
conscious effort was made to verify the Mole's 'capture' before the
parties made off into the darkness, towards bridge 'D'.

Having promised that he would not leave without 'his'
Commandos, Collier pulled away from a Mole which was swiftly
reoccupied by the enemy. With tossed grenades and close-range fire
again becoming the order of the day, the chances of the ML holding
position were slim. Nevertheless, as Collier's clear intention was still to
fulfil his promise, she continued to manoeuvre close-in rather than
seek the comparative safety of deeper water.

Next boat to attempt a landing was ML307, commanded by the
Australian, Lieutenant Norman Wallis, RANVR. Approaching the
Mole at some eighteen knots, he was greeted by the alarming sight of
burning MLs and enemy fire still pouring from positions as yet
unsubdued. With the landing place clearly in enemy hands, it would
therefore seem that his must be the first boat to have made it this far
relatively intact: but the 307 was not equipped to force a landing, for in
addition to Captain Bill Bradley's seven-man demolition team for lock
gate 'C' in the South Entrance, she carried only Captain David Paton –
the second of the Commando doctors – his medical orderly, and the
press correspondent, Ted Gilling.

Able Seaman Don Croft, RANR, a fellow countryman of Wallis who
was acting as 'loading number' to Able Seaman Bert Butterworth on
the forward Oerlikon, has written of how they,

*Eventually... reached the Old Mole. The skipper brought the
Fairmile nearby, but already one boat was on fire and another
was shot up so badly and seemed to be without life. This was
right in our path. Wallis manoeuvred the 307 around the end of*

Captain David Paton.
DR. D. PATON

the Mole and endeavoured to go in on the other [upstream] side. At this time I had to leave Bert for a while and get a rope line ready to tie to the Mole. Bert was still firing at the numerous targets. The skipper nosed the ML in, but the bows became stuck in mud and stopped our progress a few metres short of the...wall. Our asdic dome below the keel, was stuck fast.

At that moment a German soldier appeared on top of the Mole and threw grenades in our direction. Fortunately that dropped over our deck or fell short, exploding in the water. A Commando officer [Captain] Bradley, on our bridge, and [Stoker] Geordie Allen opened up with Tommy Guns and took out the enemy.

As our skipper tried to reverse off the muddy bottom, the stern swung in to the end of the Mole. [Ordinary Seaman] Stan Roberts, holding the stern rope in hand, stepped onto the stone steps to find a position to secure his line. Machine-gun bullets bounced off the Mole and smashed granite bounced about the deck and wheelhouse. Lieutenant Wallis and [Captain] Bradley realised that it was impossible to make a landing and immediately recalled Stan to the boat.... The asdic dome broke away as we moved astern.

(Able Seaman D K Croft, RANR: unpublished narrative)

Targeted by bomb-throwers and under point-blank fire, the lives of all on board were clearly at great risk. A quick consultation with Bradley confirmed that a successful landing was out of the question. This being the case, Wallis hurriedly backed away from the immediate danger, his every gun firing. Croft used his line to pull a Commando from Platt's 447 out of the water. Captain Paton, responding to a call from a surface now licking with flames, attempted to pull Captain David Birney on board; but lost his tenuous grip when the boat gave a sudden surge astern.

The repulse of 307 to all intents and purposes ended the battle for control of the Mole. She may have been only the third ML in the port column of troop-carriers; but she was the last to get anywhere near affecting a landing. The failure to possess this one vital structure robbed GROUP 1 of any chance of success, allowed all the gun positions in that portion of the dockyard to continue pouring fire out into the river, permitted reinforcements to enter the battle area by means of the still intact South Entrance crossings, and removed, at a stroke, any chance of an organized re-embarkation.

No matter how thorough the planning or preparation, every operation, once it gets under way, remains in thrall to the vicissitudes of fortune. Because of the early loss of Lieutenant Commander Wood, ML443, the fourth boat in line, was now in the control of Lieutenant Horlock, an officer unfamiliar with the crew, who had not been given the chance to study the RAF model, and therefore had only a hazy understanding of the German defences. And because of the engine failure on board ML341, Hodgson's assault team, now on board ML446, was entering the harbour sixth in line, rather than at the front where, given the failure of ML447, it might yet have been able to force a landing.

Carrying the twenty Commandos who made up group 1D, the 443 missed the Mole entirely, Horlock later revealing how, blinded by searchlights and having never been told the structure was tipped by a lighthouse, he had confused it with the eastern arm of the Avant Port. Believing that he was much further south than his actual position on the river, Horlock therefore continued north until the sight of the tall gantries lining the 'Normandie' dock brought home the extent of his error. Turning short round, he made for the Mole, now clearly silhouetted to the south. But it was too late, his report describing how, on arrival,

> I then found an ML in flames blocking my way; another seemed to be firmly aground on the Southern side of the Mole. Both gun positions, and the searchlight on the Mole were in operation; my cannon shell, though apparently on the target, seemed to make no impression on them, and ammunition was running short. I could see no other MLs in position.

(Lieutenant K M Horlock, RNVR. Action report)

With the assault on the Mole having very obviously failed and, unwilling to hazard his ship 'hopelessly and uselessly', a quick 'council of war' resulted in the decision to withdraw under cover of smoke.

While ML443 manoeuvred to the north, the advisability of attempting to reinforce apparent failure was also the subject of discussion between Lieutenant Ian Henderson, the captain of ML306, and Lieutenant Ronnie Swayne, the officer commanding her demolition troops. Henderson was number five in the line, carrying Lieutenant Johnny Vanderwerve's five-man protection squad in addition to Swayne's nine-man team. He managed to identify the Mole and turn towards it – but his passage too was blocked by the burning wreckage of his predecessors. Uncertain of what to do for the best, he continued to manoeuvre under intense enemy fire. Swayne, anxious to be put ashore with his men, proposed a landing further north; but Henderson demurred on the grounds that the risk to his ship and crew was too great. Eventually the decision was made to turn for home, his Commando passengers not at all happy at being forced to 'give up' after having come so far. Their turn would come soon enough.

While Henderson had survived the worst of the enemy fire, Lieutenant Dick Falconar's ML 446, coming in behind, was not so lucky. Having stepped into the breach when ML 341 was forced to turn back, she was now carrying Bertie Hodgson's assault troops, Captain Mike Barling's medical team, and the liaison officer, Captain de Jonghe. Prior to entering the harbour, heavy enemy fire had killed Hodgson, badly wounded his party's second officer, Lieutenant Neil Oughtred, and wounded Sergeant Robbie Barron and Corporal 'Ginger' Freeman. Still determined to press on, the ML approached, but then ran through, its turning point, the Mole having been lost in the glare of searchlights. Coming round in the river east of the 'Normandie' dock, Falconar tried again: but with so much wreckage around, with the toll of wounded mounting steadily and with both his Oerlikons out of action, a landing attempt was clearly impossible. With enemy fire as ferocious as ever and Barling's team already busy above and below deck, he too set course for the open sea.

With no troops to land, Sub Lieutenant Bob Nock's 'spare' ML298, and Sub Lieutenant Wynn's Torpedo Boat, continued to push on through the tracer and burning petrol. Both would succeed in reaching their assigned operating areas, Nock in the river east of the 'Normandie' dock, where his job was to draw and return fire, and Wynn in the Old Entrance. As with ML306, their turn would come later.

Of the dozen troop-carrying MLs to enter the harbour area, a mere two had succeeded in putting their troops ashore. That seven had either been sunk already, or were soon to succumb, was the entirely forseeable consequence of pitting wooden ships against a much more powerful enemy. There would now be no re-embarkation. The few Commandos who had made it ashore were on their own – and would remain so.

Chapter Eight

A 'GIFT HORSE' FOR TROY

The attempts to put men ashore at both the Old Mole and Old Entrance were already under way even as the dust began to settle on the debris-strewn fo'c's'le of the battered *Campbeltown*.

Her bow having ridden over the top of the caisson, she was now being swept by fire from several nearby emplacements: from gun positions 64 and 65, high on the roof of the Pumping Station; from the sandbagged position 66 abeam to starboard, and from the building which carried the heavier cannon M70. To Copland the ship was a sitting duck and he thought it 'quite miraculous' that Commando casualties were not much heavier. Paradoxically, it was the Navy who suffered more as sailors continued to work the ship and keep her Oerlikons firing, the gunners standing dreadfully exposed in their elevated bandstands.

While Lieutenant Chris Gough supervised the positioning of the port iron-runged ladder, Copland,

> dashed ...through the narrow doors – gangways and well decks covered with many wounded sailors – a job to get through

HMS *Campbeltown* Saturday am: apparently harmless, she attracts many German sightseers.

Looking from the site of the Café Moderne toward the Place du Bassin. The bridge shown pre-dates the lifting bridge stormed by Newman's Commandos.

and I had to be rather rough in dragging them out of the way where they lay across the path for my chaps coming off. "Sorry to hurt you mate, but my chaps must get through here," and "For Christ's sake leave this passage clear" – eventually to the main deck and issued orders "Roderick off – Roy off" – back to the fo'c's'le deck and found troops having some difficulty with ladders bending, but helping immediately to sling more bamboo assault ladders overside. I gave them a little time and made my way back to the main deck for the Protection and Demolition parties. On the way across the deck I heard a voice, "Major Bill, Major Bill" and going across to near the hole in the deck I found John Proctor crumpled up and bleeding badly from a leg wound. I said, "Hang on John, I can't stop now but I'll come back to you as soon as I can," – back amidships to issue the orders "Denison off – Hopwood off – All Demolition Parties off".

(Major W O Copland, DSO: unpublished narrative)

As the various Commando parties pushed forward through the hail of fire, the complementary deployment of *Campbeltown's* crew added to an overall impression of frenetic activity. The ship had struck a mere four minutes after the 0130 target, and to best support Copland's disembarkation, Beattie was withholding his orders to cease fire, stop engines and abandon ship.

Captain Bob Montgomery met with Copland before making his own way forward, accompanied by Sergeant Jameson. Having ordered the badly wounded Etches to make his way to safety, he now found himself in sole charge of all demolitions in and around the 'Normandie' dock.

With the majority of targets lying west of the caisson, the only Commandos to disembark over the starboard side were Lieutenant Johnny Roderick's Assault Party. With Lance Corporal Donaldson having already been mortally wounded, the total number of men to land was thirteen. Scrambling down ladders and ropes, Tommy-gunners to the fore, they made short work of position 66 before sweeping on to the roof-mounted M70 and bombing it into submission. Finding position M10 already knocked out by fire from Leading Seaman MacIver's 3-pounder during ML160's supporting bombardment, it only remained to silence gun 67 and a searchlight beyond, before Roderick could apportion his team for the purpose of clearing the whole of the area south of Ressort 8. Delayed action incendiary devices had been provided for the purpose of blowing up the fuel stores; however, despite all attempts to insinuate these through ventilation shafts, the precious liquid refused to ignite.

With Roderick busy to starboard, Captain Donald Roy's assault troops were quickly over the port side and racing towards the Pumping Station. Originally totalling fourteen, this party had also been reduced by casualties, perhaps the most critical loss being that of the very badly wounded Johnny Proctor. Lance Sergeant Don Randall, who, along with so many others had marvelled at Copland's astonishing display of 'sang-froid', made his own way forward carrying a bamboo ladder,

> when I got down myself, I was told to take it to the pumphouse where it was needed. When we got to the other end, [Private] Johnny Gwynne was waiting to put it up against the wall. But it had been shot through on the way across [the caisson], so he put it up against the wall, put his weight on it and about five feet came off! So we worked round the back of the building, saw three Germans running down the steps and took a pot at them. Sergeant Challington had a Tommy Gun, so he was detailed off by Roy to cope with those, but his gun jammed and they got away. Well we didn't know if they'd [all] left or not, but we eventually got to the top. Having got to the top it was like a sort of heavenly peace and I remember whistling the theme

SITE OF U-BOAT PENS

SAINT NAZAIRE BASIN

'FRIGO'

OLD ENTRANCE

SOUTH ENTRANCE

OLD TOWN

PENHOËT BASIN

RESSORT 8

'NORMANDIE' DOCK

from Snow White "It's off to work we go... ." It was absolutely peaceful there, tracers floating across the top of all of us, in different colours, but not aimed at us. It must have been about the safest place in St-Nazaire at that moment.

(Lance Sergeant D C Randall, DCM: taped interview)

While Don placed his charges on gun 64, Donald Roy took care of number 65. Some idea of the degree to which these guns dominated the approach to the caisson can be gained today by climbing up to the pedestrian-accessible roof of the enormous Old Entrance bunker, constructed in the wake of the raid to give protected access to the Saint-Nazaire Basin. Had their fire been better directed, the story of the disembarkation might well have had an altogether more tragic conclusion.

With the roof-top guns destroyed, Roy's party swept westwards across a quayside which in 1942 opened directly onto the Old Entrance, but today lies buried beneath the ferroconcrete mass of the bunker. Their destination was the all-important Bridge 'G', the single physical link between Copland's parties, Newman's HQ and the Mole. Taking what cover they could find at its northern end, they established the bridgehead they must now hold until all the northern parties withdrew. Placed as it was at the very edge of the Basin, their position was open to murderous short-range fire not only from the ships backing and filling within, but also from troops on the roof of the U-Boat complex opposite.

In the wake of Roderick and Roy came the demolition teams and their protectors. With the closest gun positions knocked out the caisson had become rather less lethal, the only unknown quantity, in the shape of the tankers, *Schlettstadt* and *Passat*, lying within the dry dock itself. Ironically, these were the ships in search of which Lieutenant Tom Boyd had sailed his *ML160* upstream. They might or might not have crews on board who were willing to fight. Fortunately, they remained for the moment, silent and dark.

A total of forty-one men, split into five 'demolition' and two 'protection' parties, made it into the shadow of the Pumping Station. The northern groups faced a lonely and dangerous passage towards the far caisson. Here, on the doorstep of the Penhoët Basin, it would be Lieutenant 'Bung' Denison's job to prevent the enemy from interfering with Lieutenants Purdon and Brett as their parties destroyed, respectively, the northern winding house and northern caisson. Had the other landings gone to plan, they might have been sharing their exposed peninsula with the parties of Burn, Pennington and Jenkins: however, the latter two were already dead; and of Burn's gallant band, only he appeared to have made it through the chaos surrounding

ML*192's* destruction.

Immediately to port of *Campbeltown* Lieutenant 'Hoppy' Hopwood's men would keep the enemy at bay while the myriad demolition charges were laid, by Lieutenant Chris Smalley at the southern winding house, and by Chant, deep within the bowels of the Pumping Station. Had *Campbeltown* for any reason failed to hit her target, provision had been made for Lieutenant Burtinshaw's party to destroy the southern caisson. Robbed of this particular purpose, all but Private Jimmy Brown were now sent northwards to reinforce Brett. As instructed by Montgomery, who knew that the effect of the main charge would be all the greater were the caisson to be filled with water, Brown laboured alone in the shadow of the destroyer's bow to place his blasting charges against the structure's outer face.

With the Commandos successfully disembarked, Beattie was free to order his gunners to cease fire, to activate scuttling charges and to abandon ship either forward onto the caisson, or over the destroyer's port quarter onto the waiting ML*177*. On descending to the main deck, he explored the ship to make sure no one would be left behind who was still alive. Oddly, he did not make contact with Copland, who,

> *searched for Beattie... . First to the main bridge – a shattered mass of twisted wreckage – up higher to the top bridge – no sign of Beattie. Down again and aft, calling his name. I ran into a party of sailors carrying more ladders for their own disembarkation but could get no information from them concerning him. Time was flying and my job only half done and I visualised troops returning to the Old Mole to re-embark and I, whose second task was to organise and control the re-embarkation, missing, so I turned to searching the ship for wounded. I managed to get them, including John Proctor, over the side and sent them down with sailors to the MLs loading up with the naval personnel near to the dock gate. John appeared to be badly hit in the thigh and had lost a good deal of blood – fortunately I had tied some rubber tourniquets round my waist before the show and so was able to put one on his leg before, literally, throwing him over the side – all my efforts to carry him down our bent and battered ladders having failed.*

(Major W O Copland, DSO: unpublished narrative)

With the wounded clear and all his parties in action, Copland then disembarked with his own team of four. Finding that Corporal Beardsell had been wounded, he sent him off with instructions to make sure Proctor got onto the gunboat: then he set off along with Corporal Cheetham, Lance Corporal 'Jock' Fyfe the radio operator, and his batman Private Gerry Hannan. His original orders had been to make directly for the Mole: but with Roy still heavily involved with the enemy, Copland chose instead to circle northwards and approach HQ along the Quai des Frégates. As the party made towards Brett's caisson, they learned from Hopwood that all appeared to be going well at the Pumping Station. This good news was, however, tempered by a failure to establish signals communication which was to bedevil the remainder of the operation. Copland himself describes how,

> *we stood in shadow and watched the crews of the ships in the dry dock running aboard. All this time Fyfe was trying to contact HQ on his set – "Copland calling Newman, Copland calling Newman". The call droned on and on, with pauses for Fyfe to say "No reply Sir, can't hear a sound". All through our movement, Fyfe continued his efforts to establish communication and... at our hottest moments under fire that calm voice went on "Copland calling Newman".*

(Major W O Copland, DSO: unpublished narrative)

In Copland's rear, Smalley was finding that the placing of charges is never quite an exact science. His small party had raced along the side of the camber only to find their access to the interior of the winding house barred by a stout steel door. Bombardier Johnny Johnson having failed to shoot the lock off with his Colt, the prowling Lance Sergeant

Gerry 'Tanky' Bright spotted a small window which they all got through. Charges were swiftly attached to the winding wheels and their motors, following which Smalley sought, and received, permission to fire from Montgomery. The percussion igniters were pulled with great expectation – but absolutely no result: Montgomery recalling how, when the failure was reported,

> *We went against all demolition principles, which is that if an explosive doesn't go up, you leave it for half an hour before you go back to it. But (Smalley) was straight in to see what was happening. And the second time it went up and showered an ML alongside with debris.*

(Lieutenant Colonel R K Montgomery, MC: taped interview)

With the southern winding house burning fiercely, attention turned to Chant and his

Private Gerry Hannan.

110

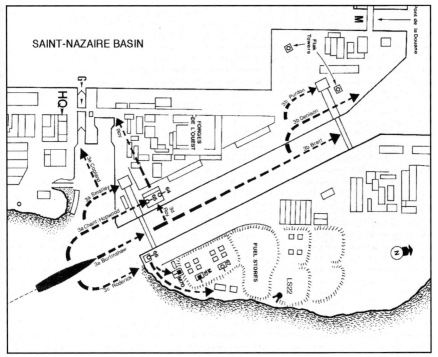

Group 3 Plan of attack.

team of four Lance Sergeants from 1 Commando, now lost to view deep within the heart of the Pumping Station. Under Hopwood's protection all five men had made it to the structure although, on arrival at its strong steel doors, there had been a moment of confusion when these were unexpectedly found to be locked. Appearing out of the gloom, Montgomery had blown them open with a small magnetic charge, following which Chant's party, escorted by Hopwood, had rushed inside and made for the iron stairs leading down into the blackness below.

With such a dangerous descent ahead Chant decided to leave the wounded Chamberlain on the upper floor, the other members of the team now carrying his heavy rucksack in addition to their own. The metal stairs which ran steeply down were connected to a confusion of galleries in such a way as to make rapid descent impossible; nevertheless they found the four impeller pumps, each of which was connected to an electric motor on the main floor, high above. Working by the meagre light of torches, in the knowledge of their absolute vulnerability to grenades tossed down from above, they took some

111

Lieutenant John Proctor,
5 Troop, 2 Commando.
PETER COPLAND

twenty-minutes to place charges on each of these and connect them ready for firing. As it was now no longer necessary for them all to remain, Ron Butler and Bill King were sent up first with orders to collect Chamberlain and get clear, following which Chant and Dockerill pulled their igniter pins and also made for the stairs, Dockerill in the lead, with Chant behind, clinging to the sergeant's belt. A fuze delay of 90 seconds hardly covered the long climb through the darkness: nevertheless they made it outside just in time, Montgomery again coming to their rescue by ensuring they took cover well away from the danger posed by falling masonry.

Having destroyed the pumps the job of Chant's team was nonetheless incomplete, for there was still the question of the four huge electric motors. On re-entering the badly damaged structure they were relieved to find that the explosion had been much more devastating than anticipated, its force having collapsed a portion of the main floor and knocked the motors off their mountings.

As the various explosions rent the night air they were music to the ears of Newman, trapped with only a handful of men in his small HQ enclave south of Bridge 'G'. That he had landed in the full expectation of finding support is evident from his account, which confirms how he had,

> fully expected RSM Moss and the Reserve had safely settled themselves in and around the HQ building. We didn't take long in coming up to the building and I went round to try to find an entrance. I don't know who was the most surprised when on turning the corner of the building I literally bumped into a German. Before I realised who or what he was, his hands were up and he was jabbering fifteen to the dozen. I called up Tony Terry who asked him in German where he'd come from. He had just come out of this building which was a German HQ! Our HQ! "Were there any more of you inside?" "Yes". "Well go in and tell them to come out with their hands up!" In he went, but almost at once the entrance to the building became very unhealthy. A quick-firing gun from a vessel in the inner Bassin had seen us and was firing at point-blank range – something like

Smalley's target, the south winding hut (left of picture), showing the broad socket into which the south caisson could be wound to allow ships to pass through.

The Old Entrance, looking towards the Loire from the area of Bridge 'G'. The building in view is the Hôtel des Ponts et Chaussées, chosen by Newman as his HQ ashore.

seventy yards away. We had to beat a hasty retreat under cover of the building. There was no sign of Moss and the reserve... .

The Headquarters area was a bit hot at this time – fire was coming from one or two vessels in the inner Bassin who were sailing backwards and forwards in the restricted area giving the dockside all they'd got. Two gun positions, on the roof of the U-Boat bunker and a tall building just by it [the 'Frigo'] *were bringing heavy plunging fire to bear all about us, and salvoes of shells from a battery on the south of the river kept on bursting overhead. At this time I was very relieved when TSM Haines and a party of the Special Task Group arrived on the scene. Haines had a 2" mortar with him with which he took on the gun positions on the U-Boat shed. His firing was grand, and for a while the firing stopped from the enemy guns.*

(Lieutenant Colonel A C Newman, VC: unpublished narrative) Condsidering the strength of the parties which should by now have landed at the Old Mole, the lack of clamour from the Old Town area was ominous: however, until such time as physical links could be established with other groups, Newman must fight on in a communications vacuum compounded by his failure to establish

contact with anyone over the airwaves. Just as was the case with Copland, Newman had his own signals expert in the form of Sergeant Ron Steele, who throughout the action on shore had been switching his set alternately from 'Call' to 'Receive' in hopes of raising Copland, Ryder – anyone: but it was hopeless. The sets so carefully 'netted in' prior to departure, were dead and would remain so.

Curtis having brought the gunboat alongside the northern wall of the Old Entrance, where she would shortly be joined by both the MTB and the out-of-sequence ML262, she immediately became the focus of attention for sailors and wounded who had got off over the destroyer's bow. Ryder describes how, as they berthed,

the remaining survivors of

RSM Alan Moss, HQ Troop, 2 Commando.

Campbeltown's *crew rushed on board. I looked for some of her officers but could find none. Someone told me that the Captain and First Lieutenant had been killed but I doubted that and climbed on to the jetty to investigate. As I did so MTB74 came in and reported for Orders. I had in mind sending [Wynn] to torpedo* Campbeltown *if plans there had appeared to miscarry and so told him to wait alongside.*

Some very badly wounded men were carried down as I came up the steps and a grenade or fuze fell between the gunboat and the jetty and burst close to me. The decks were crowded and it wounded one or two men. There was a sinister burning smell and for a moment I was afraid that our ship was on fire. It soon cleared, however, and I continued on my way to Campbeltown.

A challenge from a crouching figure with a Tommy gun halted me abruptly. I gave the password, which was my own name, and was permitted to continue. I reached the side of the dock entrance and hailed the Campbeltown, *but all seemed quiet. There was a small fire burning still in the fo'c's'le mess deck. The ML [177] we had sent alongside her had shoved off and there seemed to be no sign of life. I stepped forward and hailed again but was greeted by a burst of fire which I imagined came from one of the ships in the dock. It struck the masonry of a small hut close by me. I dodged behind the hut and watched* Campbeltown *from there for what seemed to be a good five minutes. Then to my relief I saw a series of small explosions along her port side and it sounded as if there were others on the further side too. The ship had ridden over the torpedo net and was firmly held by the bow. However, she started to settle by the stern and so I decided that everything was going to plan there. My next task was to see how the other landings were getting on.*

(Captain R E D Ryder, VC., RN : unpublished narrative)
For Corran Purdon, whose target was the northern winding house, the disembarkation had been a relatively straightforward affair, over the bow where Tibbits and Gough were holding onto the ladders. Corporal Bob Hoyle had fallen into the smouldering crater in the foredeck, Corran recalling how:

We pulled him up, burnt, and he landed unperturbed and cheerful. The ladders were unsteady, and some of us, myself included, jumped most of the way down, stumbling under the weight of our heavy rucksacks as we landed. Our little party consisting of myself, Corporals Johnny Johnson, Ron Chung,

Bridge 'G' today, viewed from the Old Entrance bunker roof. Roy's bridgehead was to the right of the bridge. The lock gates in view are those torpedoed by Wynn.

Bob Hoyle and Cab Callaway, rallied together and made our way at a trot along the side of the dry dock towards our objective... . Our rubber-soled boots were almost noiseless. We wore, for recognition purposes, webbing belts and anklets scrubbed white. En route Corporal Johnson was hit and wounded. We came to our winding house and found it had a heavy metal door. I tried unsuccessfully to shoot the lock in, then Ron Chung burst it open with a sledgehammer.

Once inside, following the drill we knew so well, we laid our made-up charges and connected them up. Corporal Johnny Johnson, in great pain, showed a wonderful example of fortitude, determination and efficiency. The other three...were cool as ice and as cheerful as if on a holiday. When we were ready to blow, I sent Ron Chung across to Gerard Brett's party to tell him we were ready when he was... . Ron Chung ran across under intense fire, fully illuminated by the glare of searchlights. He returned after successfully completing his mission having found the area swept by a hail of bullets and he himself being hit.

(Major General C W B Purdon, CBE.,MC.,CPM:
List the Bugle pp 33-4)

116

For Corran's party there had been at least a semblance of shelter from enemy fire. But for the troops spread out along the caisson, exposure was the order of the day. With the loss of Pennington had gone any chance of assaulting Bridge 'M' and the Caserne des Douanes, the failure leaving that structure's roof-mounted cannon untouched: and with the loss of Burn's troops had gone the blocking position, east of the caisson, which had been designed to forestall enemy attacks from the main body of the shipyards. With the exception of Denison's five-man protection squad, this immensely vulnerable area was therefore held only by demolition troops neither armed nor trained for the purpose.

The plan for the destruction of the caisson, whose formidable scale still inspires awe, involved placing explosives both outside and inside the structure, the latter to be achieved by entering its vast interior through hatches mounted proud of its upper surface. Unfortunately, with that same surface being used as a roadway, access proved to be impossible, every attempt to blow a passage through coming to naught.

Lieutenant Brett and his seven men from 12 Commando had been first upon the scene, joined later by Burtinshaw and his team from 5 Commando. With time speeding past, and attempts to force the hatches growing steadily more violent until such time as they were finally abandoned, attention then switched to creating as much external damage as could be achieved with the available resources. Corporal Bob Wright, who was still up with the party in spite of a shell splinter lodged in his knee, takes up the story, describing how he and Bombardier 'Jumbo' Reeves,

> got up there, found the manhole – we were on the far end of the caisson, towards the oil tanks – and we then found that we couldn't get the manhole cover up with whatever tools we'd got; and I shouted to Brett that we were going to use two limpet charges to see if we could shatter the top of this bloody big manhole...and...I detonated these charges and they never made any impact at all.

> By this time there was rifle, or machine gun, fire coming off the tankers in the dry dock: and Brett had been hit by then, because I went back to report that we couldn't get down inside the caisson...and...he was propped up by the side of this crane very adjacent to where the caisson would have been drawn back. And I didn't realise how badly he was hurt. And then he said: "Well can you get under?" Because you could get under the road: there was a gap where the road was carried over on a steel

structure and you could get under and clamber about...and put the explosives wherever we could see anything that was vulnerable, and then take the fuze up to the ring main. And (after this) I made my way back...and scuttled under cover, and that's where Blount was, and he'd been hit, and Burtinshaw had been wounded... .

(Sapper Corporal R E Wright: taped interview)

Although Burtinshaw's arrival had effectively doubled their strength, the efforts of the caisson party were being constantly undermined by the volume of fire directed against them. Copland, who was passing at the time, has recorded how:

Fire of all sorts was pouring from the high buildings on the other side of the basin [the Douaniers complex], *and the dock roads seemed light as day.*

As already noted by Wright, the tanker crews had finally plucked up the courage to fire on the caisson; in addition to which the failure of the other parties to land had left the lightly-armed demolition troops at the mercy of enemy parties closing in on them from either side. The scene was later set by Sergeant Frank Carr, of Burtinshaw's team, who in a letter to Stuart Chant described how:

We came under an extremely heavy attack with fire from...our rear, ships in the Penhoët Basin, from the east of the dry dock and also from a tanker in the dry dock. This was probably attracted by the firing of the charges by Burty in his attempt to gain access to the interior of the caisson. The laying of the charges, ring-main etc, for the outer demolition had been

The south caisson, looking east. The building centre rear was the location of flak position M70. Gun 66 was on the quayside above the floating barrier.

Bridge 'M', the Caserne des Douanes and the railway yards. The U-Boat pens have a completed first-phase roof. Two of the three gun positions can be seen on the Caserne roof. I.W.M. C3317

virtually completed when the attack came. It was so heavy we were forced to take cover briefly, Burty, myself and some others, under the decking of the caisson. We then nipped onto the dockside and engaged the tanker...with our pistols which as you can imagine was pretty ineffectual. The protection party silenced the tanker and we returned to our task. I never saw Burty again. After checking to make sure our ring-main had not been damaged, I tried to locate Burty and was told he had been killed and was alongside a nearby wall. .

119

I suppose it could be said I took over at the time. I checked for damage. We then had another attempt to open the hatch, but without success. Time was passing and we should have been ready to 'blow'. The fact that we could not complete the whole task caused some concern and I realised we would have to blow the underwater charges only. About this time a runner [Chung], arrived to say the winding house party was ready. I...removed the pins from the igniters. The resultant explosion...was heavier than intended because we had incorporated both parties' charges. I then walked the caisson to estimate damage. I could hear running water at both ends and realised it was damaged, probably enough to move it on its seating.

(Sergeant F A Carr, DCM)

The blast from the direction of the caisson was the signal Purdon and his party had been waiting for. He writes that:

The noise of firing was terrific and the place continued to be lit up by searchlights and the fire of explosions. Gerard Brett's party came through us having suffered heavily. Gerard, badly wounded, was carried by Corporals Bob Wright and ['Fergie'] Ferguson. Once they were through and clear, from what we all hoped was a safe distance, I pulled the pins of our igniters. It was a memorable sight. The entire building seemed to rise several feet vertically before it exploded and disintegrated like a collapsed house of cards.

(Major General C W B Purdon, CBE., MC.,CPM:
List the Bugle p34)

With Burtinshaw, Sergeants Beveridge, Ide and William Ferguson, and Lance Corporal Stokes all having been killed, the remnants of the various northern parties came together close by a burning building prior to withdrawing to what they believed would be a waiting fleet of MLs at the Mole. Not included in this group was either Copland or the indomitable Micky Burn. Having by some miracle got across Bridge 'G', having avoided enemy parties and at one point suddenly woken up to the fact that he was absently carrying a live grenade with the pin removed, Burn had eventually arrived by the flak towers his party had been detailed to destroy. It is almost impossible to conceive of the fact that he had not made contact with friends along the route; nevertheless, as he writes of his perplexing odyssey,

I saw no one, not even the group detailed to wreck the 'Normandie' dock's northern caisson, whom I was supposed to be protecting. There seemed to be no guns on the towers my group

were to destroy, but I went up one to make sure, though I now had nothing to destroy them with. It was some thirty feet high and had sleeping quarters for a dozen soldiers at the top. I came down with several Reichswehr jackets and a vague thought that they might be useful; then remembering that wearing enemy uniform could deprive me of combatant status, I dumped them.

I awaited Morgan and his group's arrival to demolish the swing-bridge [M] to the mainland. Prowling round a pill-box at this far end of our battlefield, I had a sense of someone prowling on the other side. Colonel Newman had given us a password which few Germans could have got away with: "War Weapons Week". I gave it and Bill Copland replied. He told me that our operation had succeeded...and it was time to begin withdrawal to the boats. He gave no news of Morgan's group or the remainder of mine. After he had gone I waited a short while longer, then started to return the way I had come...

(Michael Burn, M.C., *Turned Towards the Sun* p 138)

As to Copland's rather less lonely odyssey he and his party pressed on in the hope of finding someone to report on progress by Bridge 'M'. But the only force present there was the enemy, whose fire continued to hound them as they attempted to return to Bridge 'G' via the Quai des

A primary target of the raid was this impeller pump now replaced by more modern equipment. Plans are to refurbish it and put it on display.

Frégates. Finally driven from the main dock road, they;

doubled back and tried to get round the buildings. Twelve-foot walls barred our way and time was flying so I decided to chance the Basin road again. Bunching together, we ran and dodged from cover to cover and managed always to keep one jump ahead of the machine-gunners...

(Major W O Copland, DSO: unpublished narrative)

Having always had in mind the orders which required him to take charge of parties arriving at the Mole, Copland and his team had made good time, distancing themselves rapidly from Burn, Purdon and the parties still struggling at the inner caisson: in fact they were almost within hailing distance of Roy when, according to Copland:

Suddenly a roar of sound cracked into our ear-drums, followed immediately by a collossal burst of continuous yellow fire to our left rear. With relief I realised that it was the big Dock Pump House demolition going up and thought, "Good! that's three jobs done – the Gate, Dock Operating Gate House and Pump House." We pressed on towards the bridge at 'G'.

(Major W O Copland, DSO: unpublished narrative)

Chapter Nine

A GAUNTLET OF GUNS

The route of withdrawal for the northern parties was via Bridge 'G', thence to the Mole. Having been deeply involved with their own tasks they knew little of events on the Loire, and Newman was in no position to enlighten them. Intelligence vital to the planning of their next moves might have been expected from the southern parties; but of the officers landed there no one had been seen save Watson, and his story was precise only in relation to the increasing evidence that the ML457 parties were on their own.

Having found the Mole apparently free of enemy troops, the parties of Watson, Walton and Pritchard had pressed westwards through the Place de la Vieille Ville in the confident expectation that reinforcements could not be far behind. In order to reach Bridge 'D', they must traverse this deadly rectangle of open ground, flanked on one side by sheds and workshops, and overlooked on the other by the tenements of old Saint-Nazaire. Constructed on slightly higher ground the latter, known locally as the 'Petit Maroc', was a warren of narrow streets into which the enemy was free to feed troops for as long as the bridges over the South Entrance remained unblown.

On entering the square from the east, Watson recalls how 'a strange spicy smell brought home to me that I was in a foreign country'. A group of French civilians attempted to make contact and had to be dissuaded by warning bursts from his Tommy gun. This firing alerted nearby enemy who soon pinned him down, machine-gun bullets clanging into a litter bin above his head. His account of what happened next catalogues not only the hoplessness of the parties' position, but also the growing realization that the GROUP 1 plan must, after all, have failed.

> Not wishing to be riddled like the litter tin, it seemed wise to withdraw. I quickly rose to my feet and ran swiftly back. Luckily Wickson [Lance Sergeant Lionel Charles] saw my blue recognition pinpoint light signal before he opened fire and thanks to my rubber soles the Germans did not hear my withdrawal until too late.
>
> We found Philip's demolition team taking cover in the lee of some railway trucks. But Philip himself was not there. I was upset. [Corporal] George Wheeler told me that they had seen him fall while running across Old Town Square under fire and that he was probably dead. As the square was being raked by

Captainerie

Bridge B

Bridge D

South entrance

Old Town

Power Station complex

Santé Maritime

more than one machine gun I understood why they had failed to follow him. I was reluctant to cross that bullet swept open space myself.

If I had known then that Philip had not been killed outright but was making his way alone to his objective I would have acted differently. In the event I shouted Philip's name. The only answer was the clatter of more machine-gun fire. I turned to speak to [Lance Sergeant] Dick Bradley, but he fell backwards shot through the lung by a machine-gunner on a rooftop. I bent to give him an injection of morphine from a ready prepared syrette. I was straightening up when I felt a heavy blow on my left buttock... but I was able to walk and there was no time to dwell on the matter. Decisions had to be made.

Obviously we had to move from this exposed spot and we would have to leave Dick Bradley. We had been told to leave the wounded if they impeded the rest. We laid him under a truck hoping that it would give him some protection from the bullets ricocheting in all directions. The rest of us moved into an alley and stopped in the shadow of a shed.

(Dr W H Watson, MBE.,MC: unpublished narrative)
As there was no sign of the other parties, Watson attempted to summon reinforcements with his Very pistol; however this had been damaged and would not fire. While Wheeler made his way to Newman's position to report, Watson led the remaining troops to the right with the intention of approaching Bridge 'D' via the Quai Demange; but this route was blocked by an enemy ship in the nearby Saint-Nazaire Basin. Forced ever northwards, he decided to follow Wheeler and petition Newman directly, the Colonel sparing him two Tommy gunners to reinforce yet another attempt on the bridge. Fortunately, this almost certainly lethal enterprise had to be abandoned when a runner arrived with orders to prepare for re-embarkation instead.

Not accounted for in Watson's description of events, is Captain Pritchard's small demolition control party which succeeded in making it to the eastern side of Bridge 'D'. As they sheltered behind a small concrete hut the realisation dawned that they alone had made it. Carrying only small 'opportunity' charges there was little they could do to the bridge: however they did succeed in sinking two small tugs moored next to the Quai de la Vieille Ville. At this point Pritchard split the team, taking Corporal Maclagan with him on an exploratory circuit of the Old Town, while Corporals Shipton, Deans and Chetwynd remained to do such damage as they could to the primary targets.

Pritchard and Maclagan reached the area of the Power Station without meeting any other parties. On attempting to make their way back through the narrow streets of the Old Town, Pritchard had the misfortune to reach a corner at the same time as a German coming the other way. As recalled by Maclagan:

In one second the two of them met, in the next Captain Pritchard had fallen backwards. I took a couple of paces towards the German and emptied the remainder of my Tommy gun magazine into him. At this moment I was not aware of how Captain Pritchard had been struck, but on thinking of it later he could only have been bayonetted, as I am sure no shot was fired. I dropped down beside him to see what I could do. He was breathing terribly heavily. After a little while he spoke and his words were, "That you Mac? Get back and report to HQ. That's an order." He never spoke again.

(Corporal I L Maclagan: unpublished personal narrative)

As Maclagan made his way back to Newman, the situation at Bridge 'D' was deteriorating rapidly. As there was little the three Corporals could do, they sought cover; however this served only to put them in a new line of fire and Chetwynd and Deans were quickly killed. Now the only man remaining, Shipton wisely decided to make his way north as well.

Collier, meanwhile, was determined to hold position off the Mole.

Crew of ML *443* post-raid. The CO, Lieutenant T D L Platt, DSO, RNR, is seated centre. To his right is Petty Officer Motor Mechanic Harry Bracewell, DSM, RN. To his right is Ordinary Seaman Frank Folkard.
FRANK FOLKARD

As he pulled back from the slipway there was the sensation of the hull hitting the bottom; but what was actually being felt was the shock of grenades landing all around them. During this period the boat's twin-Lewis jammed and on Collier's instructions Able Seaman Dyer made an abortive search for any weapons that might have been left below. He had no sooner returned than a grenade dropped into the bridge, severely wounding Collier in the leg, killing one rating and wounding another badly in the stomach. In spite of his injuries Collier nevertheless remained in control, ordering his battered vessel out towards what he now hoped would be safer waters mid-stream.

The trials of this ML characterized what had by now become a brutal battle for survival out in the fairway. Stephens' ML192 and Tillie's ML268 had already been destroyed; Platt's ML447 was on fire and Irwin's ML270 had been disabled by damage to her steering gear. Collier's ML457, Fenton's ML156 and Falconar's ML446 had all suffered significant casualties; and of the port column, a total of four boats, MLs 307, 443, 306 and 446, were already withdrawing. The gunboat, soon to be joined by MTB74, was stationary in the Old Entrance, not far from where Rodier, in ML177, was taking off *Campbeltown's* crew. Boyd, in ML160, was searching abortively upstream for *Passat* and *Schlettstadt*: while Sub Lieutenant Nock was manoeuvring so as to draw fire in the fairway between the fuel stores and the Pointe de Mindin.

Having strayed upstream, Burt's ML262 and Beart's ML267 had gone about and were now en-route for the

Lieutenant Tom Boyd CO of ML160. T.W BOYD

landing places. Beart nosed his ML onto the foreshore with the intention of disembarking Moss and his precious 'reserve'. Manoeuvring under fire, a number of men did actually make it over the bow: but they were recalled almost immediately and the ML began

Crew of ML *262*. Seated centre is Lieutenant Edward 'Ted' Burt, DSC, RNVR, CO of *262*. Seated to his left is Sub Lieutenant 'Robbie' Roberts, RNVR. E.C.A. ROBERTS

to back away towards deeper water. Heavily hit, she started to burn and the order to 'abandon' was given, some survivors taking to a Carley float, the remainder milling around in water ripped by bursts of machine-gun fire. In reporting the loss, Newman writes of how,

> *their ML had been hit and they had to abandon ship in midstream. Getting a number of the swimmers onto a Carley Float, Moss had started paddling for shore, but gave up his place for another survivor, taking to the water himself and towing the Carley Float along. An enemy machine gun opened fire on them and poor RSM Moss gallantly gave his life trying to save the others.*

(Lieutenant Colonel A C Newman, VC: unpublished narrative) Most of those on board were killed, Beart being numbered amongst the eleven lost from a crew of sixteen: of the eleven Commandos, only three survived to become POWs. Included amongst the materials which went down with the ship were the special rockets with which Newman had planned to signal his outlying parties to withdraw.

More immediately fortunate was Lieutenant 'Ted' Burt, whose ML262 had led Beart back down the river. In a report written while still a POW, he recalls how they came in under *Campbeltown's* stern and:

Sergeant Gerry Taylor, HQ Troop, 2 Commando ML 267. PETER COPLAND

Made fast alongside about 0140 and landed troops. Power House [in fact the Pumping Station] *and other buildings in vicinity of dry dock then blown up shortly after our troops disembarked. Came under heavy fire from flak trawler backing and filling in Saint-Nazaire basin. Replied with forward gun, which fired about eighteen rounds and then irrevocably jammed. Carried on with two stripped-Lewis guns from bridge on cannon mounted between bridge and funnel of enemy craft. This gun was twice silenced by our Oerlikon and Lewis fire. Then, in accordance with previous arrangement with Lt Woodcock...we cast off and manoeuvred stern first to Old Entrance lock gates to tow them shut preparatory for demolition. Saw one military party running back to disembarkation point with wounded and went back alongside to pick them up.*

(Lieutenant E A Burt, DSC.,RNVR: draft action report)

ML262 had berthed alongside the north wall of the anchorage.

Securing bows in, the parties put ashore had been Lieutenant Mark Woodcock's nine-man demolition team and their five-man protection party under Lieutenant 'Dick' Morgan. But the Commandos' sojurn ashore was short-lived, Morgan claiming to have seen, and responded to, the signal to withdraw. With the boat alongside again, they clambered back on board whilst Sub Lieutenant 'Robbie' Roberts held the painter ashore.

Having cast off for a second time, Burt was in the process of turning the boat when another party of Commandos was seen to be heading their way. This was Smalley's retiring party, which had seen in the ML an accelerated means of escape. As described by Burt, he,

Stoker Len Ball, DSM. ML 262. LEN BALL

> *went alongside again and picked them up. Enemy trawler in Basin again opened fire. We cast off and turned by* Campbeltown's *stern. Forward gun completely out of action and abandoned. Army officer [believed Lt Smalley] killed trying to bring this gun into action against advice of 1st Lieut. Was then hit by cannon fire in funnel, aft and in engine-room at deck level, starboard side aft.*
>
> (Lieutenant E A Burt, DSC.,RNVR: draft action report)

The last hits had knocked out the after gun and its crew, and set fire to the after magazine: however, with power still available and steering intact, there was every reason to believe a successful withdrawal could still be made. Continuing his report, Burt writes of how they,

> *carried on at full speed until abeam of Old Mole, where [ML457] lay disabled by gunfire about a cable off. Went alongside her intending to take her in tow, her captain [Lieut Collier] was on her bridge and said he had abandoned ship, but refused to be taken off himself, advising us to get clear as by then both ships were under fire from a heavy gun on far side of St Nazaire Basin. Rang down full speed ahead, but had only got about half a cable away when we received direct hits on bridge, engine-room, and mess deck. About five Army on bridge either killed or severely wounded.*
>
> (Lieutenant E A Burt, DSC.,RNVR: draft action report)

This really was the end. The engine-room was on fire and the engines

131

and telegraphs out of action. The upper deck was being raked by machine-gun fire. The wounded Stoker Len Ball was sent aft to rig the tiller steering: but it was all to no avail and the order to abandon was given at around 0245, the ship blowing up some thirty minutes later.

The loss of the two ships left many survivors struggling in the same stretch of icy water. In his attempt to reach the 'safety' of midstream, Collier's boat had been hit on the starboard side and set on fire. On receiving the order to 'abandon ship', a single Carley float had been tossed over the side. This began to drift seawards with the ebbing tide taking with it a handful of survivors, the last to join being Collier himself. Of his crew the number killed would eventually amount to eight out of fifteen: and of Burt's crew, seven were to die out of sixteen. It was a loss rate of fifty per cent: and it was still only the beginning for the 'little ships'.

Manoeuvring around the destroyer's stern, Burt would have passed very close to the point where Rodier's ML177 was evacuating about thirty of *Campbeltown's* crew, including Beattie, Tibbits and the remainder of the doomed ship's officers – Lieutenant Chris Gough, RN, Surgeon Lieutenant Winthrope, RCNVR, Mr Hargreaves, RN, the Gunner (T), and Warrant Engineer Locke, RN. The intake included many wounded, who were cared for by Winthrope, with Hargreaves assisting.

Having come alongside at 0145, the ML was clear to begin her run downstream by 0157, now with almost fifty people on board, her own crew supplemented by Sub Lieutenant [E] Toy, RNVR, and POMM Rafferty, RN, of Stephens' 20th Flotilla base engineering staff. As she worked up to twenty knots her success thus far seemed to be giving the lie to Rodier's conviction that he would not survive the night.

So as to be free of their topweight, Rodier fired his two torpedoes at ships anchored south of the Avant Port. They were almost clear of the estuary, when suddenly struck in the engine-room by radar directed fire. Frank Arkle was in the process of lighting a smoke-float when the first shell struck. He recalls how:

Men started launching the Carley floats from either side of the bridge. They did not secure the painters and the floats were out of sight with no one aboard before anyone could stop it. Rodier and I were astern of the bridge discussing what to do next when the second shell hit, and I vividly remember the funnel folding apart as if in slow motion. Rodier was between me and the blast so the poor chap took the brunt. I was hit all down my left side, from foot to face.

(Sub Lieutenant F W M Arkle, RNVR: account prepared for author)

Petty Officer Motor Mechanic Rafferty recalls: 'lying on the engine-room deck almost submerged in water and in complete darkness.' He climbed up to a deck 'overflowing with dead and dying and hardly anyone unscathed.' Several batteries were shelling the boat yet amidst the horror of it all, one crew member was still returning fire. Rafferty then went below again to see if the engines could be restarted; but they were clearly finished. A fire began in the galley and quickly spread amidships. Tibbits was one of those who tried valiantly, but hopelessly, to douse the flames, Beattie writing that, after this

> as he was talking to Chris Gough, a burst of machine-gun fire
> came and killed them both instantly. I was more fortunate as I
> had been standing with them only a few seconds before, and had
> moved off to talk to some ratings.

(Lieutenant Commander S H Beattie, VC.,RN:
letter to Mrs E Henderson, 28 June 1945)

With the boat beginning to break up amidships, the decision was made to take to the water. The struggle to save her had been intense and she was not finally abandoned until about 0500. Five of the crew did not survive, this number including Rodier – just as he had predicted – and Toy. As no record was kept of the intake from *Campbeltown*, it is impossible to be precise about losses. Beattie would survive, as would Warrant Engineer Locke: however the loss of Gough, Tibbits, Hargreaves and Winthrope was bitter reward for the magnificent effort

The northern quayside of the Old Entrance, which saw Ryder step ashore from MGB *314* has disappeared under the mass of the bunker. The armoured firing ports are clearly visible top right.

put into placing their old destroyer right in the heart of the enemy stronghold.

To stand on the heights of the northern shore today, it is almost impossible to conceive of the dangers this tranquil stretch of water once posed to Ryder's fleeing ships. Compressed as it was between Sperr Feuer Zones 'Casar' and 'Berta', it was a miracle that any boats got through at all – a miracle diminished only by the dread coincidence that those which did not were the ones whose decks were awash with survivors.

Having laid his special torpedoes against the outer pair of Old Entrance lock gates, Wynn was ordered to make for home with a party of *Campbeltown's* survivors on board. Powering away from the anchorage at about 0220, the MTB's maximum speed of forty knots offered the prospect of a swift and safe passage out. However, when Wynn chose to power down and pick up two men from a Carley float which suddenly loomed out of the darkness, the little boat's advantage was lost and she became just one more easy target. Even though it had been Wynn's intention not to delay for a second in hoisting the men on board, it was still too late and the shells which had been dogging her progress finally hit her square.

The blast of the hits spelled both the end of the boat and the beginning of a tragedy which would slowly unfold through the long, cold hours of the night. Now heavily on fire there was no alternative but to abandon ship, which Chief Motor Mechanic Lovegrove was about to do when he noticed Wynn was nowhere to be seen. Recalling Lovegrove's actions in 1945, Wynn writes of how he,

> *fought his way through the flames to look for me down in the wheelhouse where I had been blown by the force of the explosion and was almost unconscious. He took hold of me and got me up on deck and then, putting his arm round me pulled me into the water himself and swam with me to a Carley float. We were in the water some twelve hours, Lovegrove supporting me by lashing me to the float or by holding onto me and undoubtedly, if it had not been for his total disregard of his own life and suffering, I would not have survived.*

> (Lieutenant R C M V Wynn, DSC.,RNVR:
> report: 22 February, 1945)

For most men, safety appeared to lie in the float towards which Wynn was being pulled by Lovegrove. Estimates of the number crowded around this single refuge range as high as thirty, although no reliable figure for the total number on board the MTB exists. All that is known for sure is that of this struggling mass of humanity, only three would survive to be picked up eventually by the enemy.

Starkly illustrating the vagaries of a fate which seemed to strike with neither pity nor reason, was the experience of Lt Irwin's ML270 which, manoeuvring south east of *Campbeltown's* ramming point, was being hit continuously by small calibre fire. At about 0140 a heavier shell struck her stern, the explosion knocking out the hydraulic steering gear and leaving Irwin with no alternative but to circle while attempts were made to rig the cumbersome auxiliary system aft. Very much a 'sitting duck', the *270* nevertheless seemed to lead a charmed life until a form of control was re-established. Then, with orders being passed by voice from Irwin to the hand steering position, this enormously fortunate ML was able to limp away. Almost unbelievably, she had not suffered a single serious casualty.

Of ML160, her companion in the Forward Striking Force, there had been no sign during this period. Having entered the harbour off *Campbeltown's* starboard bow, Boyd's Hotchkiss gunner, Leading Seaman MacIver, had engaged and knocked out gun position M10 on the foreshore of Roderick's target area. Then, with the destroyer securely in position, Boyd had taken the boat up-river in search of tankers, unaware that *Schlettstadt* and *Passat* were safely ensconced within the 'Normandie' dock. Disappointed that they were nowhere to be found, he came about with the intention of going alongside *Campbeltown*, noticing, and silencing en route, a Bofors battery mounted on top of a power house.

MGB314's forward pom pom, with Able Seaman Peter Ellingham sitting on barrel, and Able Seaman William Savage, minus beard, far left. P. ELLINGHAM

Having got clean away with this bombardment, Boyd then took the opportunity to torpedo an anchored ship, although only one of his 'fish' actually ran. At that point things began to really heat up with the ML, held by searchlights, being hit repeatedly. The deck petrol tank, which Boyd had had the presence of mind to fill with sea water, was pierced several times, and a blinding crash amidships caused engines and lights to cut out – though thankfully only for a moment. Judging it wise to be rid of his remaining torpedo, he fired it in the general area of the town and pressed on doggedly towards the dry dock.

In the area where *Campbeltown* was sinking steadily by the stern, there was no sign of the gunboat. With the radio still dead, and no new orders forthcoming, Boyd therefore decided to rescue whomever he could – a decision which was to prove the salvation of many on board the foundering ML447 which, having been hard hit, was on fire and drifting helplessly off the tip of the Old Mole while efforts were being made to get the many wounded off onto a Carley float. Of her Commando party only David Birney, Lieutenant Bill Clibborn and TSM Hewitt were in a fit state to swim: and of these Birney too would be lost following Captain Paton's failed attempt to pull him on board the withdrawing ML307. Responding to a call of 'ML ahoy!', Boyd saw her burning and came alongside, placing his own boat between 447 and the Mole.

Still under intense fire, the 447 was cleared of the Commandos and crew who were still alive and three men were plucked from the water. Having got under way again, the 160 was hit several times aft, knocking out one engine, causing a fire to break out in the tiller flat and wounding several of those on board. Telegraphist S E Drew reported that a shell had actually passed between him and his radio set. Cutting power to his one remaining engine, Boyd then conned the ML towards the open sea, skilfully winding his way through the huge waterspouts thrown up by shells from Dieckmann's heavier guns, a number of which came far too close for comfort. So determined was he to get his crew and passengers back to England, that Boyd had decided to steal a fishing boat should this prove necessary: however, with luck still favouring his battered ML, the port engine was finally got going again and by 0330 they were on their way home at last.

By around 0230 it was time for the gunboat to go to the support of the remaining embattled MLs, Ryder recalling that, on coming out to look at the Mole:

> There were two MLs lying off unable to get in, in face of the fire from the pill box on the jetty and also from the housetops. Our 2pdr Rolls Royce gun aft was out of action and so were both our 1/2" twin turrets but our excellent Pom-Pom Gun layer,

136

Able Seaman Savage, opened an accurate fire on these positions.
One of the MLs [was] hit by tracer where she lay but we
succeeded in silencing the pill box. The other ML moved in to
take advantage of this but accurate fire from a flak position
further back in the town hit her repeatedly and she also burst
into flames. There seemed little that we could do. We couldn't see
any other craft afloat. Up and down the river there seemed to be
about seven or eight blazing MLs and so we decided to go back
into the Old Entrance to make contact with our forces ashore and
let them know the situation.

(Captain R E D Ryder, VC.,RN: unpublished narrative)
During her time out in the fairway the gunboat had been hit
repeatedly, though not yet fatally: so the decision to return to the
anchorage, especially with so many wounded already on board, held
within it a huge element of risk. Ryder's account of what they found
there illustrates both the danger and the ever-shrinking range of
options open to him:

Matters were without doubt getting out of hand now. There
was a fierce battle going on across the Old Entrance. It was
impossible for us to go in. We were unable to join in this battle
as we were unable to see which was our own side. Somebody,
presumably one of our own side, climbed back on board
Campbeltown *and poured a fierce fire from one of the Oerlikon*
guns into the general confusion. He was shot and fell from his
gun. There seemed to be little that we could do here, we were
loaded down with over forty men, mostly seriously wounded. We
were floodlit by the blazing building close by, and lying stopped.
Being the only ship left, we were attracting the individual
attention of all hostile positions that could see us. Most of the
tracer from close range passed low over our heads but we must
also have been clearly silhouetted to the Bofors Batteries on the
south bank as they again opened an unpleasantly accurate fire.
We could see it coming straight at us, an unpleasant feeling. But
they seemed to be shooting short and it mostly struck the water
and ricochetted over our heads. We lit and dropped a smoke
float. While crouching on our bridge, I held a hurried council of
war with Curtis and Green. The situation was undoubtedly
deteriorating – in a few minutes we should inevitably be set on
fire like the others. Both of the only landing places were in enemy
hands and sadly we realised that there was nothing we could do
to help our gallant soldiers on shore. We had many wounded on

*board, our decks were crowded with them so that it was difficult
to move. We must leave at once and save them.*

(Captain R E D Ryder, VC.,RN: unpublished narrative)

At 0250, with the 'sputtering and sparking' smoke float holding the
enemy's attention, Curtis sped seawards. Passing the still-burning
Sperrbrecher, she was soon caught again by probing searchlights and
the shellfire that followed the beams. In the area of Les Morées tower,
a withdrawing ML – probably ML*156* – was met and passed, the
gunboat laying a trail of smoke to help cover her passage. Of the move
from the area of Mecke's flak guns to that of Dieckmann's heavier
batteries, Ryder notes that:

*Whereas the tracer from the flak positions invariably passed
astern of us, the coastal artillery on the other hand must have
overestimated our speed as their salvoes landed ahead. Great
plumes of water rose up ahead of us, leaving a column of thin
misty vapour which must have helped to conceal us. Gradually
the searchlights lost us, first from the north bank and then from
the south, but the guns continued to fire at us for some time.The
last salvo of all straddled us in the dark at a range of about four
miles.*

(Captain R E D Ryder, VC.,RN: unpublished narrative)

Almost out of danger now, the gunboat reduced speed so as to allow
the trailing ML to catch up. Suddenly, out of the darkness came an
enemy patrol vessel whose crew opened fire at close range before
hauling off into the void once more. Yet again the gunboat seemed to
have got away with it, with no immediate reports of significant
damage. It was only when Able Seaman Frank Smith attempted to
train the pom pom fore and aft and discovered it wouldn't budge, that
gunner Savage was found to have been killed – a tragic end for a man
who, up to that very last moment, had come through his numerous
engagements unscathed.

Given the confusion and lack of ship-to-ship communication, Ryder
probably had every justification in thinking the gunboat was 'the only
ship left' when she pulled away from the Old Entrance. Yet even as he
made for the Mole, Sub Lieutenant Bob Nock's ML*298* was
approaching from the north east on completion of her patrol between
the oil stores and the Pointe de Mindin. In sailing towards the heart of
the action, Nock was intending to make his ship available to
Commandos wishing to withdraw. He ran past *Campbeltown's* stern
and, finding no sign of life in that quarter, made for the Mole only to
find the approaches blocked by burning wreckage. Returning to the
Old Entrance he managed to berth alongside the southern quay, only
to find that this area too was deserted. Ringing down for full

revolutions, he then sensibly decided to make for the rendezvous point, passing the northbound gunboat en-route, but receiving no orders from her: indeed, Nock does not even appear to have been spotted.

On passing the Mole, the *298* was illuminated by the flames of burning boats, coming under sustained fire at close range. She caught fire aft as her transom was set alight by burning pools of petrol. Eventually struck by heavy shells, and in spite of making smoke, both engines were knocked out and the majority of the crew either killed or wounded. By this stage south of Les Morées tower, Nock ordered the drifting boat abandoned before the flames reached as far as the petrol tanks. Two Carley floats were put over the side; however, of a crew of sixteen, only six men remained to take advantage of them.

The loss of the *298* brought the total of small boats destroyed in the harbour and estuary to nine -more than fifty percent of the seventeen which had made up the attacking formation. Of those now attempting to rendezvous with the waiting destroyers, MLs *306, 307* and *443* were relatively unscathed, while the gunboat, plus MLs *156, 160* and *446* had all sustained varying degrees of damage and were carrying casualties. Of this number, ML*156* was steering erratically by hand tiller, as was the otherwise very fortunate ML*270*.

Having left harbour well in advance of schedule, the surviving boats' timetables no longer complemented that of the escorting destroyers, which quit their offshore patrol at 0420 to begin a long sweep eastwards towards point 'Y', twenty miles from the estuary

Below the main gun positions of the Fort de l'Eve, is a broad platform giving access to the interior of the old French Fort. During the raid this would have presented the Germans with an ideal firing platform.

mouth and the first position at which they might hope to meet retiring MLs. Reversing their course at 'Y', *Tynedale* and *Atherstone* would then push west, along the withdrawal course of 248 degrees, to point 'T', at which position it was judged safe for the MLs to turn north for home.

Pushing ahead of the other retirees, Henderson's ML*306* reached point 'Y' too early and, anxious to put distance between themselves and the enemy shore, pushed on alone towards 'T'. Emulating Henderson, though some way behind, MLs *160, 307* and *443* came together as a unit and also pushed west into the comforting darkness. Of the remaining four boats, MGB *314* was now escorting, at greatly reduced speed, the erratic ML*270*: while Falconar's ML*446* spent some time accompanying the equally slow *156*. Passing through 'Y' much later than the others, this group of four stood by far the best chance of being swept up as originally planned.

With *Tynedale* and *Atherstone* known to be close by, the crews of the small boats could take some comfort from the fact that friendly warships were out there, somewhere. However, these were not the only formations making for the general area of the rendezvous points; for Schmidt's flotilla of five torpedo boats, despatched the previous evening to patrol along the port's approach routes, had been recalled at 0250 and was even now steaming shoreward at maximum revolutions. Consisting of *Seeadler, Jaguar, Iltis, Falke* and *Kondor*, each roughly equivalent in size and power to *Tynedale* and *Atherstone*, these far outclassed the straggling remnants of Ryder's little fleet. Of even greater concern was the fact that their position, when recalled, now put them on a course almost exactly the reverse of the British line of withdrawal.

Chapter 10

A SHOCK OF ARMS

The success of the GROUP 3 withdrawal plan rested on Donald Roy's ability to hold his tenuous bridgehead for more than an hour, Newman having scheduled Bridge 'G's destruction for zero plus seventy-five to give the northern parties time to get clear.

Situated directly north of Bridge 'G', his twelve men were horribly exposed to fire from the various structures which lay along the western edge of the basins. First amongst these was the U-Boat complex, a mere 175m away: directly to the north of this lay the gun positions on top of the Caserne des Douanes; while to the south of pen fourteen was the Entrepôt Frigorifique ['Frigo'], whose two roof-mounted cannon were only 250m from the all-important bridge.

Further complicating matters were the various ships which, manoeuvring in the Saint-Nazaire Basin, were acting as very effective mobile gun batteries. But for the despatch of Schmidt's flotilla in response to Kelbling's sighting report, their number might have included his five destroyer-sized torpedo boats: as it was, they consisted primarily of four relatively lightly armed harbour defence vessels from the Saint-Nazaire *Hafenschutzflotille*, and five more

Quadruple 20mm cannon on top of the 'Frigo' (Entrepôt Frigorifique). Overlooking the Saint-Nazaire Basin, with the roof of the U-Boat pens visible in middle of the picture. The view is across to the Old Entrance: the Hôtel des Ponts et Chaussées can be seen through the gun barrels.
COLLECTION : SCHARPFENECKER. - DROITS : LIBRE/CLICHÉ ECOMUSÉE DE SAINT-NAZAIRE

substantial minesweepers from *Korvettenkapitän* Marguth's *16. Minensuchflotille*. On receiving news of the landing, the captain of one *Hafenschutzboote* scuttled his ship to prevent its capture by the enemy; while the latter formation, which had been moored beside the Quai Demange, moved across the basin to protect the pens and the U-Boats being serviced within them.

With the estuary and the western edge of the basins under German control, Newman's men were effectively trapped within a crude figure-of-eight whose circles touched at 'G'. Adding to this lateral compression were the parties of German troops which soon began to push towards the centre, aiming to isolate the Commandos as close as possible to their landing areas.

Early in the action, these were primarily 'scratch' units cobbled together from personnel immediately available, their job being to pressure the invaders until such time as regular *Wehrmacht* formations could be rushed to the port's defence. Within the pens themselves, the crews of the U-Boats having been withdrawn to 'pasture' in and around la Baule, security became the responsibility of armed and helmeted technicians and artisans. Available to the Harbour Commander ('Hako') were the *Hafenwachkompanie*, assigned to port security and defence, and the *Hafenüberwachung*, or Port Police. With so many installations to be guarded, the crews of the various ships not directly involved in the defence were also put to use. From the north, moving along either side of the Penhoët Basin towards Bridge 'M' and the inner caisson, were Numbers Two and Four Works Companies –

View north from the roof of the U-Boat pens towards Bridge M and The Penhoët Basin.

again technicians and workers acting in an emergency role as infantry: while pushing across the South Entrance, via the bridges assigned to GROUP 1, were assault groups formed from those amongst Mecke's Flak Battalions 703 and 705 not immediately involved in serving the guns. In the process of being mobilized well out to the west of the port, was *679 Regiment* of the *333rd Infantry Division*. This was the formation which, because of its equipment and training, was to be feared the most: however, it would take time to assemble and deploy, this brief delay leaving Newman a narrow envelope of time during which he might still exploit what remained of his dwindling initiative.

Pinned as they were behind the dubious shelter of a low wall, casualties amongst Roy's party were inevitable. Indeed, on viewing their position from the roof of the U-Boat pens today, it is almost impossible to conceive of how any survived at all. Lance Sergeant Don Randall was hit by a ricochetting lump of metal before Roy, who was out by himself close to the point where the tenuous bridgehead was approached by the main dock road, called him over to join in the anxious wait for signs of movement amongst the shadows. Private Arthur Ashcroft, who had lost his helmet when he fell part way into the

Private Arthur Ashcroft.
MRS M. ASHCROFT

smoking hole on *Campbeltown's* foredeck, pretty much sums up how it was for those who were left when he describes how he and Lance Corporal Harold 'Aggs' Roberts were,

> *Lying down the bottom of this wall, and this ack-ack gun was having a go at us: and I must have counted four or five shells passed over the top of the wall, and I had no tin hat on. I didn't know what to do. One hit the top of the wall and the next one must have got me. But what I got in the head, he got in the legs.*
>
> (Private Arthur Ashcroft: taped interview)

Pushing south towards Roy's fire-swept stretch of quayside, Copland describes how, having just made it across an open stretch of ground,

> *I saw, about 40-yds away, dim figures moving and thought "This should be Roy's party, so here goes", pressed my torch with its dim blue light and called "Copland here" – an answering blue pinpoint of light blinked back at me and a voice called -"Roy here – come through". I stopped a few seconds with*

Syrette, containing morphine of the type used on the raid. The glass cap when broken exposes a needle with which the injection may be administered.

Donald whose men were all disposed under what cover they could get from the heavy fire and told him I was pushing on to the Old Mole. Motioning to my party to move, I got half way across the bridge when a burst of MG fire cracked into the 12-ft high concrete walls at the side of the bridge. A strong hand pulled me to the ground and an even stronger voice said "Keep your bloody head down". We lay on the roadway till the fire slackened, during which time I called out to my party to check their names. Cheetham, who had been with us at the last gap, did not answer so I crawled back to see him lying this side of the gap, about 40-yds away. I arranged with Donald to have him sent down with one of his own wounded, [Private] John Gwynne. Time was flying far too fast and I still had visions of fourteen beautifully empty MLs waiting at [the] Old Mole...so, collecting Hannan and Fyfe close behind me, we upped and made one final dash for the shelter of the buildings on the "home" side of the bridge at G.

(Major W O Copland, DSO; unpublished narrative)

Also moving south through Roy's position was Micky Burn, who speaks eloquently of both the hoplessness of the embattled 'Laird's' position and the courage with which it was being maintained, writing of how:

Moustachioed, bonneted and kilted, his was the kind of stance and situation would-be Beau Gestes have dreamed of and Donald probably never given a thought. Possessed of both calm and brio, all he needed was bagpipes and a few more men. I went on "through" and came upon a sprawled soldier, dreadfully wounded in the head and in great pain. I gave him a morphia injection -- some of us had been issued with the kit – and prayed that I had done it correctly.

(Michael Burn, MC: Turned Towards the Sun p139)

He had indeed done it correctly, for the soldier was Arthur Ashcroft, and he would eventually recover. His northern odyssey complete, Micky then crossed safely into the HQ perimeter, where new adventures awaited.

The badly wounded Etches had stopped with the bridgehead party for a time, before withdrawing slowly across Bridge 'G'. Purdon's party crossed with rather greater dispatch, he having decided simply to; 'make a bolt for it and trust to God.' With the structure being regularly swept by machine-gun fire, Chant's party took the rather more extreme alternative of crossing underneath. Montgomery too crossed under the bridge, though on reaching the 'home' side he was to find Jameson missing, he having presumably been hit during the attempt. Of the remaining northern parties, most followed Purdon's approach, while a few, seeing the amount of fire that was coming in, decided instead to go for the outer pair of Old Entrance lock gates. It was by this means that Corporal Bob Wright, along with Corporals Joe Molloy and 'Fergie' Ferguson eventually brought the wounded Brett to safety. Having begun his own withdrawal at 0230, Roderick's isolated party was amongst the last to come through the bridgehead before it too was pulled back to the relative safety of the south side of the lock. Most of his party crossed over the now deserted hulk of *Campbeltown*, he himself being hit on his way to 'G'.

Defying the odds had cost Roy heavily. Of the twelve who made it ashore seven were wounded, two of these – Privates Ashcroft and McCormack – severely. It was a remarkable feat of arms marred only by what amounts to the murder of Private Johnny Gwynne. For, having helped Cheetham across 'G', he was to find there a group of the enemy who disarmed them both and then attempted to kill them. Gwynne was shot in the back. Cheetham, somehow, managed to escape and reach HQ.

As the various parties came in Newman was at last able to build a picture of events in the GROUP 3 area. To Micky Burn, who in moving independently towards the Mole would certainly have been captured but for his knowledge of German and the timely intervention of Haines, he was 'wonderfully calm'. Assisted still by Wright and Molloy, Brett came in to report and after a 'well done' from the Colonel, was placed in a warehouse with others whose mobility was now in question. As the group south of 'G' began to swell, Copland's report that,

> all had been well with the Campbeltown *and the wounded was a great relief to me. This meant that the time seemed right to withdraw Donald Roy and his bridgehead and to pull back to the Old Mole area. My rockets had gone down with poor old Moss's party, so I had to get a message to Donald by runner. Lance-*

Corporal Harrington went off with the message, having to cross and return by the bridge, which was by now under very heavy fire. I'm afraid I had a very gloomy picture to tell Bill about his re-embarkation scheme as I could see nothing in the harbour but burning MLs and the chance of getting the chaps away was fast disappearing.

(Lieutenant Colonel A C Newman, VC: unpublished narrative)

The return of Copland's party brought Lance Corporal 'Jock' Fyfe together with Sergeant Ron Steele, the two radio operators now combining their efforts to raise anyone out on the boats. But with the continued silence came the realization that their warm and comfy rides home had either left the area or been destroyed. Having been through so much already, the loss was deeply shocking. Landed as part of what had seemed like a successful assault on the Mole, 'Tiger' Watson was appalled when he reached the shore again and saw that,

the surface of the water was lit up brightly by sheets of flaming petrol while thick oily black smoke rose above the flickering glow. A few blackened hulks, some still smouldering redly along the waterline, were all that remained of the MLs to take us home. Those vulnerable craft that had been unable to land their soldiers, now battered and laden with wounded and dead, had at last reluctantly made for the open sea. Our transport had gone.

We stood speechless. For a moment all seemed suddenly silent to me despite the guns which were still firing down the river.

The Old Mole looking seawards, viewed from the approximate position of the Commando assembly point prior to their breakout attempt. At the time of the raid the structure would have been surmounted by two bunkers.

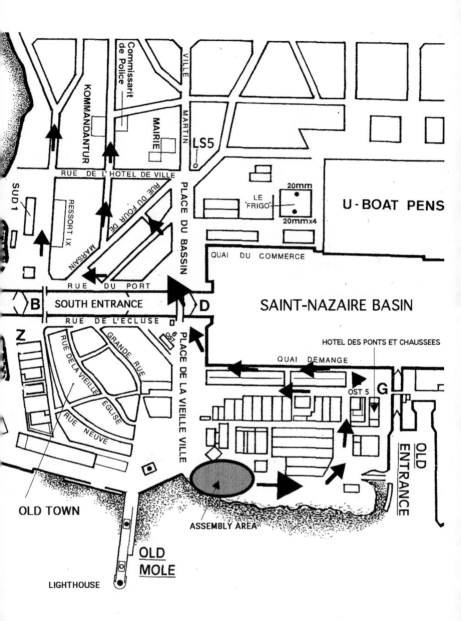

ROUTE OF ATTEMPTED BREAKOUT

147

Bridge D from the defenders' point of view. On the far side is the Place de la Vieille Ville. Somehow the Commandos managed to force their way across and break right towards the seafront.

Presumably shock had rendered me unconscious of sound for those few seconds. But there was no time for contemplation. Major Bill was already organizing a defensive perimeter.

We got Wickson's Bren to bear on that thrice cursed gun on the Old Mole which I had originally thought to be safely in our hands. Its crew were the very men who had been running with arms raised and whose lives I had spared. They had crept back and done untold harm to my comrades since then.

(Dr W H Watson, MBE.,MC: unpublished narrative)

As the officer in charge of the supposed 're-embarkation', Copland has recorded how he received from Newman the,

news that my beautiful picture of fourteen empty MLs was but a dream and that they were mostly sunk or burned out. I told Charles that I would push on to the Old Mole where our troops would be assembling. He said that he would come with me and the whole party withdrew through the empty dock warehouses...

Our hoped for re-embarkation point and its background looked like a scene from "The Inferno". Close in to the Mole, the shells of nearly burnt-out MLs still glowed red on the river, whilst in the night behind them and seemingly suspended in mid-air, blazed a sea of burning petrol through which came shells

148

and tracer fire of all kinds, some of the shells exploding with a
rather futile little "crack" in the air just ahead of us.

(Major W O Copland, DSO: unpublished narrative)

For the close to one hundred men who were coming together some
way north of the base of the Mole, on the shoreline close to what is
today the Avenue Saint-Hubert, the sight was indeed dispiriting – but
it was not necessarily the end. Many were wounded, ammunition
could not be replenished, and all too many – the demolition troops –
had nothing to fight with save grenades, pistols and sheer bloody-
mindedness. Now much more open, much of it occupied by the
Ecomusée, the area they faced then was dark and forbidding, packed
with sheds and workshops, and criss-crossed with railway lines on
which sat goods wagons, singly or in leaderless trains. With the sea
aflame behind them, the bridge at 'G' surrendered to the enemy, and
the Place de la Vieille Ville swept by machine-gun fire, it had all the
characteristics of a trap – save acceptance by those apparently caught
within it that there was no way out. It was a time for leaders: and of
those the Commandos had talent aplenty, Copland's aggressive
response capturing the general mood:

A quick succession of thoughts streamed through my mind.
"Can we hold this position until all our troops get back again?"
"What will Charles decide to do?" "We can't just give in
without making a fight for it, whatever the odds against us are."
"Can we pinch a ship and get away?"

Donald Roy came in with his party. I told him to throw a
protective screen around our right flank and told Haines to do
the same for our rear and the little house near which we had
assembled. Firing broke out close at hand, enemy troops were
trying to penetrate to within bombing range, but they were
quickly repulsed by our Tommy-gun fire. Charles called me to
him and we had a quick consultation, deciding to push through
the town in order to make the country beyond, split into small
groups and head for Spain. I assembled all Officers, to whom
Charles explained the situation. I regrouped them and their
parties and went back to join Charles and Stan. We were
standing in the lee of a railway wagon, talking, when a German
hand-grenade came over the wagon and exploded at our feet –
not one of us got a scratch!

(Major W O Copland, DSO: unpublished narrative)

Prior to leaving Falmouth, the men had been given a lecture on escape
techniques: but it had been rather less than effective in preparing them
for an arduous trek across 500km of occupied territory – even should

they be fortunate enough to make it into Saint-Nazaire proper. Of the three bridges connecting the dockyard to the main town only one, the lift bridge 'D', at the southern extremity of the Saint-Nazaire Basin, was in any way reachable, and even that could not be approached directly. To get to it the remaining Commandos must engineer a long right-hook by way of their original HQ, then filter south along the dock and quayside roads to a position from which the eastward approaches to the bridge could be rushed. It would be a tall order for fresh troops: an almost impossible one for men tired, wounded, who were all the time aware that as they weakened, their enemy only grew stronger.

Recalling those tense, expectant moments following his realisation that that the GROUP 1 assault had failed and that the all-important bridges over the South Entrance remained intact, Newman writes of how,

> *time was too vital to attempt any detailed form of reorganisation, and the formulation of a fixed plan of action, and in making my decision to form independent groups to fight their way into the town I considered that, not only would such small parties spread over a fairly large area be able to inflict on the enemy the greatest amount of casualties, but that they would have individually a better chance to filter through the town and make their getaway into the country beyond.*

> *The scene at the bridgehead is difficult to describe, there were several railway trucks around which gave excellent cover for*

Bridge D with the Saint-Nazaire basin and U-Boat pens.

sundry groups forming the perimeter. Fires and smoke were everywhere and small arms fire was coming from most of the buildings around us. Stan dealt with some screaming Germans up an alley between two buildings close by us – Why do they scream so? Everyone was behaving magnificently and coolly returning the fire with ever decreasing ammunition.

(Lieutenant Colonel A C Newman, VC: unpublished narrative)

On Charles's orders, 'Major Bill' had crudely redistributed the troops for what would certainly be a heavily contested dash towards Bridge 'D',

with Micky Burn's party as vanguard, then Donald Roy and his men, then...the Demolition parties, armed only with Colts in the centre, with Haines and his men to bring up our rear. From Charles came "Get on. Get on" – amplified by my own voice – only too well we both knew the Campbeltown *might blow up at any minute, and we with her. We crossed the road through the deserted concrete warehouse, all the time bursts of fire coming from the most unexpected places, and turned left. Here we were checked. Micky and his party had become detached and Donald's party were held up by heavy fire. I called Haines up and told him to take his men forward, contact Donald Roy on the way and then to crash ahead with all speed. "Any questions Sergeant Major?" "None, Sir," came the reply – it seemed just like an exercise with Haines as the perfect student... .*

(Major W O Copland, DSO: unpublished narrative)

The 'separation' of Micky's party was anything but an accident, he having spotted, during his sojourn by Bridge 'M', how this route might offer an alternative means of escape. He had met, within the new perimeter, Paddy Bushe and Tom Roach, two Riflemen from his own 6 Troop who had landed successfully from ML 177 and, given the alternative of crossing to north or south of the basin, had,

decided, for Paddy, Tom and myself, on the northern end.

I had just been there and back on my own, had encountered no one and knew where cover was, had noted also that the towers that end had no guns and that the soldiers quartered on the top had left. I made another decision: having already escaped three German captors once by speaking German [en-route to the Mole]*, I would try the same bluff again if challenged a second time. Tommy guns and tin hats would give us away. I ordered Paddy and Tom to dump them and follow me. We set off on the road between the warehouses and the submarine basins. We were* *challenged. I called back, in German, "The English have landed". We strode on towards the swing-bridge which would give us access into the town and this time were fired on. Paddy and I ran into the cover of the workshops and warehouses. I looked for Tom Roach, and called him, but there was no reply. Morning began to dawn. Not far away a French or German ship was moored. It looked deserted. Paddy and I sneaked aboard and went below into the boiler-room. It seemed as good a place as any to lie up.*

(Michael Burn, MC: *Turned Towards the Sun* p140)

Back with the main column, 'Tiger' Watson remembers how 'Bung' Denison, on seeing seaplanes moored out in the river, had suggested stealing one and flying it home: however:

As dear old "Bung" had been discharged from the Air Force because of his inability to land a plane in one piece, I had no hesitation in rejecting the idea.

The main column moved up a narrow road going north towards the submarine basin. Donald Roy, scorning concealment, strode along in the middle of the road hurling grenades to right and left, his kilt swinging. It was a magnificent sight.

(Dr W H Watson, MBE.,MC: unpublished narrative)

Where the road met another a German rifleman was sniping at them, dodging back and forth from cover. Watson's Tommy-gun burst did not dissuade him from reappearing, and nor did the blast from a grenade tossed by Roy. When he popped into sight once more Watson, making for the corner as fast as he could, tried another burst with the Tommy gun – but the magazine was empty. The German fired at short range, his bullet striking Watson's left arm and breaking the bone. Given the circumstances, he regards himself as fortunate that:

The bullet that close had not developed a wobble so the bone was not shattered, just snapped, and the main arteries and nerves were undamaged. Nor did it have time to inflict a large and ragged exit wound. It was a neat "through and through". In fact it was the romantic wound of my boyhood fantasies and it stopped me in my tracks. I dropped my Tommy gun and sat down abruptly.

(Dr W H Watson, MBE.,MC: unpublished narrative)

Johnny Roderick attempted to carry him onwards, but the pain was just too great. Having injected 'Tiger' with morphia, he therefore hurried to regain his position in the van of the column. 'Hoppy' Hopwood, much to the chagrin of Watson who; 'was determined not to be taken prisoner, but to sell my life dearly if need be,' hove into view and gently relieved him of spare Tommy-gun magazines and Colt pistol, before disappearing into the darkness. As the morphia began to take effect, others in the column came past. 'We wished each other good luck as they stumbled over me and passed on. Soon I was left to my own devices.'

With parties of the enemy mixed in amongst the buildings there was no sense of territory held, only the sustaining comradeship of a drive for freedom which carried them forward through a psychedelic world of sweeping searchlights, flashing tracer and the blast and shock of grenades. Corran Purdon's words bring all this to life as he describes how:

> We were being fired on from all sides, some of it coming from very close range, but we charged on rather like a pack of rugger forwards. There was a certain amount of laughter, cursing and calls of encouragement and every now and then someone was hit. ...a lot of us had some near squeaks and I vividly recall that when I tripped on a strand of wire and had fallen flat on my face, a German bullet struck the cobbles within inches of my head, throwing up sparks and chips of stone... .

> (Major General C W B Purdon, CBE.,MC.,CPM:
> *List the Bugle* p35)

As the parties, in street-fighting formation, moved north towards the bridge at 'G' before sweeping left and back along the Quai Demange, Corran had been up with Stuart Chant, who recalls how, when Corran went sprawling, they burst out laughing – but in his case not for long, for he was almost immediately shot in the knee. Completely immobilized, he was carried onwards by Sergeant Ron Butler and Private Jimmy Brown until such time as he, realizing he was jeapordizing their own chances of escape, ordered them to leave him behind. Already towards the rear of the column, Stuart now found

View from the position of Roy's bridgehead, by bridge G, towards the 'Frigo' and the U-Boat pens.

himself alone on the cold, wet Quai Demange, propped up against a warehouse and staring directly across to the U-Boat pens. Shorn of the support of comrades, in pain, immobile and waiting to be found by the enemy, it was a horribly demoralizing end to what had begun as a great adventure: yet worse was to come.

At the southernmost end of the same quayside, the main group halted in the shadow of a warehouse. Directly ahead lay the Place de la Vieille Ville, and the German occupied Old Town; while to their right, some seventy metres away lay their target – the massive girdered bridge which led directly into the heart of the town. Freedom seemed to be but one more dash away: however, once they emerged from cover the Commandos would be at the mercy of fire pouring in from all sides. It should have been impossible; but as Newman's account affirms, he was priveleged to serve with men who, accepting no such limitations, tore across the open ground, pitting their resolution to succeed against that of the enemy to stop them.

The road leading to the bridge and the bridge crossing itself was a difficult job. I can't pick all the names of those chaps out who made the crossing possible, but outstanding among them was TSM Haines who was superb – he alone knocked out several pockets of enemy with Tommy gun and Bren gun fire. Donald Roy's leadership and coolness, Bill's constant holding together of the groups preventing what might have been easily formed splits in the party, and Stan dashing about as if he was on a rugger ground. As we made the dash across the iron bridge, the bullets were ricochetting off the girders over our heads – I fully believe the Germans had forgotten to lower their sights!

(Lieutenant Colonel A C Newman, VC: unpublished narrative)
Faced with the charging Commandos, the defenders ran. Bill Copland paused for just long enough to pump .45 rounds into the slit of the pill box guarding the far end of the bridge, then he too was over, joining in the search for the most promising-looking routes through the town. Having carried the bridge, the Commandos found themselves in Saint-Nazaire proper. Here was both a new battlefield and a new enemy, for by this time *Wehrmacht* reinforcements had reached the town and were beginning to take control. His left battledress trouser sticky with blood after being hit by a grenade, Corran Purdon describes how, having made it to the 'town' side:

A German motorcycle combination came flying round the corner [into the Place du Bassin], I pumped several rounds into the occupants who crashed, dead, into a wall. My feeling of satisfaction at what I thought was my personal success dissolved later on when I discovered that just about everyone present claimed to have fired simultaneously on the luckless enemy! Then we saw what seemed to be an armoured car, firing and moving into position at a crossroads about a hundred and fifty yards ahead of us. Seeing that the way directly ahead was barred we turned left. We split into smaller parties and I was among a group with Colonel Newman and Major Copland. We came on a lorry parked by the roadside and Bill Copland tried to get it started. All he succeeded in doing was to switch on the headlights, illuminating, among others, the Charles Atlas figure of "Bung" Denison, our protection party commander, to cries of "Put those bloody lights out!" I was at Charles Newman's side as an armoured car passed us, and then we started what has since been called "the St Nazaire Obstacle Race", clambering over backyard walls and into and out of houses. In one room breakfast was set, and if my memory is correct, "Bung" had a mouthful or two en route!

(Major General C W B Purdon, CBE.,MC.,CPM:
List the Bugle p36)

As all party commanders had been instructed to follow whichever route of escape seemed most appropriate, the HQ group was only one of many clusters now attempting to pick their way through the German cordon. With the routes to the north blocked by the 'Frigo' and

Saturday am: hopeful evadées are rounded up one by one.

U-Boat complex, this group headed south and west along streets and alleys between the seafront and the Rue Villés-Martin – a part of town which they were not to know housed the *Mairie*, the *Commissariat de Police* and the *Kommandantur*. Numbering some sixteen men and with dawn fast approaching, they were eventually forced to go to ground, Newman having determined that,

> *the time for a halt wasn't far away. Every cross road by now seemed to be picquetted with an enemy machine-gun and movement was very difficult. In the street was a house with lights in it and the thought flashed through our minds to knock up the inhabitants to ask for a chance to hide till the following evening, but this was turned down and we got into a house opposite in which we found a very convenient air raid cellar complete with matresses down into which we piled. As far as possible wounds were dressed and well earned cigarettes were smoked. A watch was kept at the stair head and I decided that here we should stay till nighttime when we would set out in pairs for the open country. I also decided that if we were found in the cellar I would surrender as the wounded were in a pretty bad way and a single hand grenade flung down the stairs would see the lot off. Sergeant Steele was at the stair head when we heard Germans in their heavy boots enter the building. We heard them go upstairs and then what sounded like them leaving again. Just as we thought we were safe, somebody shouted something in German and I knew it was all up. I dashed upstairs and tried to indicate that we would surrender. We were hustled into the street with the ignominious feeling of having our hands up and marched across the road to the lighted house – German Headquarters! and so ended our part in the affair.*

(Lieutenant Colonel A C Newman, VC: unpublished narrative)
In addition to Newman, Copland, Purdon, Denison and Steele, the captured party included Bob Montgomery, Frank Carr, Tony Terry, Ian Maclagan and the remarkable Etches. Within the headquarters there was an attempt at interrogation; but there was little conviction in it, Copland recording the words of a young officer whose conclusion was that he, 'did not expect to get any information from British officers'.

While the ever-tightening cordon swept up most of the others who had by now gone to ground – Donald Roy walking right into enemy hands while attempting to ease the lot of the wounded – some did manage to prolong their evasion to the point where escape became a very real possibility. Having made it across the bridge, George Wheeler, now in company with the Canadian, Lance Corporal Sims,

Badly wounded Lance Sergeant 'Des' Chappell, with, left to right, Private Bishop, Corporal Evans and Private Eckmann.

found a hiding place;

> *in a garden and then in a dried-up drain underneath the*
> *house. We lay there from about 0600 hrs till midnight. We were*
> *not disturbed at all. When we left our hiding place about*
> *midnight we discovered that we had been lying under the house*
> *next door to the German Kommandantur.*

(Corporal G R Wheeler, MM: action report)

Elsewhere TSM Haines led a party which sought temporary shelter in the cellar of a bombed-out building. The wounded Bob Wright was there, along with Lance Sergeant Challington, Lance Corporals Howarth and Douglas, and Private Harding. At one point they came close to capture, or worse, when searching Germans came right to the cellar steps: but after that they were left alone to plan for an escape, in pairs, as soon as darkness came again.

Amongst the most unlikely hiding places was Bridge 'D' itself, Corporal Bob Hoyle and Private Jimmy Brown having secreted themselves underneath, amidst its supporting girders. Oddly enough, neither man knew the other was there.

While most of the Commandos had succeeded in crossing, a number still remained on the dockyard side either because wounds precluded further progress, or because promising hiding places presented themselves early on. Johnny Roderick led a group, containing several wounded, which sought shelter within a warehouse stacked with bags of cement. Nestled high above the ground they were most unlucky in being spotted the following morning, their deteriorating physical condition having limited their attempts to build a concealing parapet.

With their movements now restricted only by the fear of vicious 'Tommies' lurking round every corner, German troops combed the dockyard, and began an intensive search of civilian properties in the Old Town. The process began of clearing away the sailor and Commando dead, stretcher-bearers of the local *Défense Passive* assisting in this, under German orders. Many survivors of sunken boats had already come ashore to either medical treatment or incarceration. To these were now added the more seriously wounded of Newman's men, left behind prior to or during the breakout attempt. Lance Sergeant Dick Bradley, who spoke fluent German and whose original family name had been Goebbels, recalls how close he came to being 'finished off' as he lay, helpless, the effects of the morphia combining with blood-loss to rob him of consciousness:

> *In due course I became semi-conscious again. I could hear two*
> *German soldiers near me, one saying to the other, "I'm going to*

Casualty is believed to be Sergeant George Ide of 5 Commando.

Corporal Bert Shipton, left, assists Lance Sergeant 'Dai' Davis.

let him have a bullet in case he's playing a trick on us". So the other replied, "leave him alone, he's dead". I don't think I have ever kept so still and silent in all my life.

(Lance Sergeant Dick Bradley, MM: Saint-Nazaire Society newsletter, November 1983)

In due course Bradley would be picked up by the Medical Corps [*Sanitäter*] and taken to the northern edge of the Old Town, close by bunker Ost 6, where the Café Moderne was in use as a collection point for wounded prior to their being moved out of town.

Also caught in the net was Watson who observed his three would-be captors' tentative approach with interest. Rifles at the ready they were in a state of nervous anticipation the possible consequences of which were lost to 'Tiger' in his present state of morphia induced 'pleasant lethargy'. Helped to his feet he was in the process of being searched when another group appeared whose 'prize' was the wounded Brett. Supporting each other they too were led to the cafe where they found Bradley 'lying deathly pale on a stretcher'.

The arrival of Brett had taken the sting out of the hostility initially evidenced by Watson's captors. For Chant, however, there was to be no such timely intervention when, having been joined by a young soldier from 2 Commando, the two were approached by three black-uniformed Germans, armed with machine pistols, whose obvious aggression caused Chant to freeze and to caution his companion to do likewise. Responding to shouted commands, and in spite of Chant's warning, the young soldier made the mistake of standing up, at which point he was shot dead. Saved by his immobility and only belatedly identified as a wounded officer, Chant was also dragged to the cafe where his account records the presence of Private Thomas McCormack, a badly wounded member of Roy's 5 Troop, whose tragic, bleeding figure would later be misappropriated by the Germans in support of their spurious claims of victory.

With the coming of daylight, the group within the cafe were moved outside where, as they waited for transport, their presence in full view was obviously meant to come across as a tableau of defeat. And indeed, in the cold light of morning, there was little to be cheerful about; for only a little way to the north, the half-sunken hulk of *Campbeltown* was still in one piece when, by rights, she should have blown up hours ago. Had the Germans already found and disabled the charge? Had all the fuzes failed, in spite of the sterling efforts of Tibbits and Pritchard? Whatever the reason, there she still sat, shell-scarred, forlorn... and silent.

Chapter Eleven

HARD RAIN FALLING

The approach of dawn found Schmidt's flotilla, led by *Seeadler*, steaming hard for Saint-Nazaire. Steering 040 degrees, at 26 knots, they came to 'Action Stations' at 0632 in response to the sighting of a small, barely visible, shadow to port. Having already mistaken French fishing boats for enemy ships, *Jaguar*, as tactical number 2, was ordered to pull out of line, illuminate and, if necessary, destroy.

Approaching the apparently stationary vessel, *Jaguar's* commander, *Kapitänleutnant* Friedrich Paul observed propeller wake, increased to 25 knots and switched on his searchlight. Caught in its beam was what appeared to be a British torpedo boat, easy prey for a ship as powerful

Kapitänleutnant Friedrich Paul (inset), commander of *Jaguar*, intercepted **ML306** and sought to capture her as 'spoil'.

Jaguar.

as his own. Having given the order for fire to be opened, Paul then decided to use his size to best effect and ram her.

Although he had every reason to expect a quick and easy victory, his 'MTB' was, in fact, Henderson's ML306, a boat whose Commandos were not about to be 'put in the bag' without making a fight of it. Consisting of Lieutenant Ronnie Swayne's nine-man demolition team and the five more heavily armed troops of Lieutenant Vanderwerve's protection party, their belligerent response to his incautious approach was just about to spoil Paul's day.

Lance-Sergeant 'Des' Chappell. E.L.D. CHAPPELL

Henderson had been some fifty miles out when the sight of Schmidt's approaching flotilla had caused him to cut his engines and bring the ship quietly to 'Action Stations'. With nothing more than his vessel's Lewis guns and the Commandos' Thompsons and Brens to supplement the fire of his one remaining Oerlikon, he nevertheless prepared to engage his vastly more powerful adversary, returning fire and manoeuvring the ML in such a way as to negate most of the force of *Jaguar's* impact. At any time during the ensuing engagement Paul might have used his 4.1-inch guns to bring the affair to a swift and bloody conclusion; however, as his intention now was to subdue the British vessel so that she might be taken as a prize, he continued to rake her with lighter weapons.

On board the *306* the toll of casualties mounted steadily. The after Oerlikon was knocked out. A strike on the bridge dealt Henderson a mortal wound. Vanderwerve was lost overboard, and Lance-Sergeant 'Des' Chappell badly wounded in the head. Corporal Llewellyn was killed, as was Private Tomblin and the coxswain, Leading Seaman Sargent. When Able Seaman Alder was hit, the already wounded Sergeant Tom Durrant took over his twin-Lewis mounting, directing streams of lead at *Jaguar's* superstructure in spite of all the fire directed against him. Calls for the ML's surrender were at first ignored: then, with dawn approaching and nothing to be gained by fighting on save further loss of life, Swayne at last acceded to Paul's demands and gave up the ship.

Preparing to tow his prize to port, Paul sent his own men on board the *306* and began the transfer of her surviving complement into German custody. Although care for the wounded aboard *Jaguar* was efficient and correct, no amount of medical intervention could help the dying Henderson, Petty Officer Motor Mechanic Bennett or the gallant Tom Durrant, finally shot from his guns after sustaining multiple wounds. Courageous though the ML's stand undoubtedly was, the cost of her defiance had been bitter indeed.

Having detached *Jaguar*, Schmidt had pressed on at high speed aware that he might, at any moment, intercept other British craft withdrawing. In fact his warlike credentials were very speedily put to the test when he met the westward-steaming *Tynedale* and *Atherstone* – adversaries so much a match in speed and power that, after a brief but

stinging engagement, Schmidt chose to break for home, his withdrawal later justified by claims of having identified 'from muzzle flashes' not two British ships, but a greatly superior force of six to eight.

Having beaten off the enemy, *Tynedale* and *Atherstone* resumed their sweep along the approximate line of withdrawal, the approach of daylight greatly enhancing their chances of spotting Ryder's ships. The seven attempting to run for home were at this time split into two groups, the first containing the relatively intact ML*160*, ML*307* and ML*443*, and the second consisting of the gunboat with ML*156*, ML*270* and ML*446* in attendance. Given the condition of the latter formation, with the gunboat taking on water through inumerable holes, the *156* badly damaged and the *270* steering erratically by tiller, it was indeed fortunate that they were the group sighted by *Tynedale* and *Atherstone* at 0702 on the Saturday morning.

While wounded and extraneous personnel were transferred from the vessels still thought capable of surviving the passage home, the battered *156* was cleared by *Atherstone* which ship then moved on to the gunboat, taking on board Ryder, his staff and her extensive complement of casualties. In retaining only those immediately concerned with working the ship, her CO, Lieutenant Dunstan Curtis, made one very notable exception this being the body of Able Seaman Savage which he was determined should remain with the ship for eventual burial ashore. Ryder later recalled how, when he left his 'floating HQ', she was an 'awful shambles', taking on water through dozens of holes, and with her decks slippery with blood.

The surviving vessels having got under way again, the manner in which the intimacy of affairs in the estuary was all too soon replaced by considerations of practicality rather than sentiment, found no place in Tweedie's formal description of Ryder's last hour in command of what remained of his force.

HMS *Atherstone*.

At 0752/28 a Heinkel 115 float plane was sighted and proceeded to shadow the force. As it was now full daylight, it was considered that air escort was imperative, and HMS TYNEDALE

An HE 115 shadowed the returning raiders.

therefore made a Shad report, followed by a Help message at 0756/28. At 0815/28 a single Beaufighter arrived. At 0820/28 [Ryder] *increased the speed of the force to 15 knots and HMS* TYNEDALE *thereafter acted under his orders until HMS* CLEVELAND *joined at 0857/28 and assumed command of the force.*

(Lieutenant Commander H Tweedie, RN: action report of HMS *Tynedale*, 31 March, 1942, para 23)

Missing from this stark recital of fact is a human dimension encompassing first, the end of the empty and forlorn *156* which, having survived British attempts to finish her off was finally despatched by the Heinkel: second, the total loss of the Beaufighter whose crew attacked and collided with a prowling Junkers 88: and lastly the arrival of Commander Sayer RN, in *Cleveland* who, having seniority, assumed command of the enhanced formation, relegating Ryder to the status of exhausted supernumary, deeply regretful at having been forced by events to abandon Newman and his men.

Cleveland and *Brocklesby* having joined too late to do more than escort the survivors home, the force then sought to put as many miles as possible between itself and enemy airfields. With the passage of hours Sayer became unhappy with the degree to which his damaged charges were holding him back. His patience finally evaporating around midday, he ordered the gunboat and ML*270* and ML*446* abandoned, following which they were sunk by gunfire. Having achieved so much it was a sad and poignant end much deprecated by crews who were convinced they could have brought the vessels home. By 1400 therefore, only ML*160*, ML*307* and ML*443* remained afloat of the seventeen ships which had entered the estuary. Pressing doggedly onwards these, against all the odds, would succeed in reaching Falmouth early on Palm Sunday morning.

Even as the Ryder group adapted to a world beyond the tight, empathic companionship of danger shared, the waters of the Loire were being systemmatically combed for those fortunate enough to have survived the tragedies of the night. While a few of the shipwrecked raiders had succeeded in reaching the northern shore, the majority – including many wounded – had been left to drift through a passage of hours whose physical and emotional extremes had been beyond the capacity of some to bear.

Having been hard-hit by the shell which claimed Mark Rodier's life, Sub Lieutenant Frank Arkle had entered the water from the blazing ML177, spattered all over with shrapnel. Benumbed with cold and weakened by shock and pain, he was plucked from the sea on the Saturday morning by a trawler which numbered Sam Beattie amongst its bedraggled, half-drowned harvest. Ted Burt, carried by the tide onto Les Morées tower, was picked up, as were the remnants of ML457's crew, minus the badly wounded Collier who, during the hours of darkness, had slipped away from life. For the dwindling cluster of torpedo-boat survivors, salvation would come too late for most, only Wynn, Lovegrove and Stoker Savage making it through their lengthy ordeal in the freezing water.

Brought eventually to shore, these would join in captivity the men who, having taken to the water within the confines of the harbour, had struggled earlier to various quays and jetties: the pitifully few who had made it off the blazing ML267 and ML268; the rather larger number who, like Sub Lieutenant 'Robbie' Roberts and Stoker Len Ball, had swum ashore from ML262; and the two distinct parties who were all that remained of Stephens' ML192. Of these, Stephens' group, on the Quai René Kerviler, had been speedily moved to the security of the U-Boat pens; while Sub Lieutenant Collinson and the others sheltering in the Mole lighthouse retained a form of liberty until a German party at last felt confident enough to approach the structure.

The arrival of daylight, as well as saving the lives of many trapped in the water, brought both an intensification of the search for 'Tommies' ashore and the start of a general movement of prisoners out of town, to the west. Prior to their transport arriving this was a deeply depressing time for the group who had spent the last hours of darkness in the Café Moderne. To existing wounds, only sketchily dressed, was now added the ignominy of being 'on display', 'Tiger' Watson describing how:

> There were five of us, all wounded, laid out in a row on the pavement. Gerard Brett was on my right and McCormack, a kilted private in Donald Roy's troop, was immediately to my left. Beyond poor McCormack lay Stuart Chant, a lieutenant of 5 Commando and leader, like Gerard Brett, of a successful demolition team. He had a bullet in his right knee joint. Pallid Dick Bradley lay beyond him.
>
> We must have looked a sorry sight as we all had various

additional minor wounds. Blood oozed through the bandages covering McCormack's face and a bloodstained dribble ran down from his shattered mouth. Mercifully he was only semi-conscious.

We were stared at by curious Germans. Some U-boat men came up. One spoke some English, and told us that he had been in the merchant navy before the war and had a girlfriend in Hull. "Ah, you're lucky! For you the war is over!" he added wistfully.

Then the Propaganda Kompanie came with their cameras. We tried with mixed success to look both defiant and indifferent. They moved about us and clambered over us to get the best pictures as though we were a collection of inanimate objects in a still life study arranged for their benefit.

We were now put in the back of an open military truck [their number including the badly wounded Arthur Ashcroft], lying or sitting on the floor. There followed a painful, if fairly short journey. The streets had potholes and craters over which we were jolted. Lying on my back I could see the people looking down from their open windows as we passed. We waved to them, I paying the penalty for having to let go my left arm temporarily to do so. We tried to look happier than we felt and that although we might be down, we were certainly not out. The people waved

Private Tommy McCormack, wounded in the face, is put on board a lorry near the Café Moderne.

The loading of the wounded continues. Lieutenant Stuart Chant, is seated facing camera.

back and shouted encouragement but several women, seeing McCormack's bloody head rolling about, hid their faces in their hands. We eventually got our guards to support the semi-conscious McCormack. They at least were not without compassion. That jerking, grinding journey is not easily forgotten, but it finally ended after 16 kilometres.

We drew up at an imposing building, the luxury Hôtel l'Hermitage which normally catered for the wealthy holidaymakers at the fashionable seaside resort of La Baule. Now it was a German naval hospital. We were laid out on a deep pile carpet in an enormous room festooned with imposing crystal chandeliers. Here we were reunited with the other 90 or so British wounded, soldiers and sailors...

(Dr W H Watson, MBE.,MC: unpublished narrative)

A primary destination for wounded who were to remain here for some days, La Baule was also first stop along the road to captivity for able sailors and Commandos rescued from the sea, or wrested from their hiding places by troops who nervously scoured both old town and new. Micky Burn who, bored of waiting in his boiler-room, had gone up on deck at about 1000 to have a look, recalls most vividly how:

When I saw that Germans were searching other moored ships and must soon reach us, I went back down to Paddy [Bushe] and waited. I heard them on deck. As they came clumping down the gangway to us, I pushed Paddy into a corner and covered him, thinking "For the first time I am being brave and correct and public-school. This is how responsible leaders behave in books." A couple of German infantrymen appeared with rifles and bayonets fixed. We put up our hands, I surrendered in German, and they took charge of us.

Paddy and I were marched through the streets hands-up with bayonets at our backs. French men and women made friendly gestures and, seeing that a German team were photographing us for Goebbels's propaganda, I formed my fingers into the v-sign. We met Sam Beattie, now a prisoner, wearing only a blanket.

At the moment Paddy and I met him, we were quite near the dry dock. It was past ten o'clock and there was HMS Campbeltown *still embedded in the caisson. At the latest she should have exploded an hour ago. It was hard not to show dismay, or seem in a hurry to get clear of her. We joined Charles and the rest in a guard-room, all equally on edge and trying not to show it, all wondering what the hell has happened, what has gone wrong, why has she not gone up.*

(Michael Burn, MC: *Turned Towards the Sun* p 141)

A thorough search of the warehouses turned up Johnny Roderick's group atop their partially-built cement-bag 'mountain'. Included amongst their number was Lance Sergeant Alf Searson of Walton's demolition team who, prior to the breakout, had suffered the galling indignity of being shot by one of his own side.

As the German net was steadily drawn in, Jimmy Brown and Bob

Casualties from the battles around the northern caisson lie beside the Penhoët Basin.

Casualty believed to be Sergeant Beveridge, 5 Commando.

Hoyle were extricated from within the supporting structure of Bridge 'D'. With so many parties now involved in the search it is hard to see how anyone could possibly escape their prying and prodding; and yet, as anxious minutes wove themselves laboriously into nerve-wracking hours, hopes of freedom remained alive for Wheeler and Sims in their concealing drain, and Haines, Wright, Challington, Howarth, Douglas and Harding in their cellar. For these there was only the aching wait for darkness. The world beyond that was yet an aeon away.

Even as sporadic shooting could still be heard in the streets of Saint-Nazaire, various captive groups, including that of Newman, were motored out of town, Bill Copland noting how: 'All along the route, groups of French people gave us concealed "V" signs and shook hands with themselves in joy...'. Their destination was a cafe whose population swelled steadily as more and more survivors came in. Stories were swapped and friends were reunited, the relief and comradeship promoting an atmosphere which, in spite of their grim and heavily armed guards, Copland describes as becoming ' merrier and merrier until an observer might well have said, seeing us – "I can't imagine what you find to laugh at" – reaction, I suppose.'

From the various reports, Newman and Copland were able to piece together a tale which spoke of much success; yet all were conscious that there was still missing the central core of their intelligence, which was of *Campbeltown's* planned eruption. Given the degree to which her fuzes were susceptible to the effects of cold, damp and shock, their stated delay was as much a function of chance as of intention. It is Ryder's considered opinion that, all the other fuzing arrangements having been shot away, the ship's explosion became entirely dependent on the long delays: and it was the casual approach of these to timekeeping that was fraying so many nerves as Saturday morning wore slowly on towards noon.

By 1100 local time, the process of bringing in prisoners and collecting bodies was well in hand. The trawler which had plucked so many survivors from the water having deposited them within the area of the Avant Port, Beattie, clad, as Burn has recorded, only in a blanket, was led off to be questionned not far from where his ship had become an apparently harmless object of curiosity for crowds of Germans and their civilian hangers-on. His passage unobstructed by any other British ships, *Kapitänleutnant* Paul brought *Jaguar* into port, adding the sailors and Commandos of ML*306* to the growing throng awaiting transport out of town.

The experience of Madame Loreal, at the time of the raid a young woman about to be married, exemplifies the distress and confusion of a civilian population caught up in events which would ultimately destroy the lives and homes of many. Having spent the night with her family in the cellar of their building on the northern edge of the Old Town, she had returned to bed, frozen, at daybreak, only to have the doors of the apartment thrust open by Germans searching desperately for 'Tommies'. The position of the building affording her an excellent view towards the Mole, she could see that while the Germans had been careful to move their dead out of sight of the populace, a decapitated corpse remained by the gun position on top of the pilot house. Other bodies, some kilted, were being thrown into a lorry. Towards midday she went out with a friend, recording how dazed and distraught civilians 'kept themselves to themselves, wearing their identity cards which were necessary to move about and pass over the bridges.'

They were close to the Mole, comparing notes on the terrible events of the night when, at about 1130 local time, the fuzes on board *Campbeltown* finally detonated the huge mass of Amatol. The violence of the explosion rent asunder the whole forepart of the ship, blasting

HMS *Campbeltown's* bow is fully astride the caisson. Gun postion M70 can be seen in the background.
This view illustrates the vulnerability of Copland's Commandos to the guns on the Pumping Station roof.

steel and other, often human, debris high into the air, and hurling out a shock wave which tore across both town and river. Despite being more than 400m away from the caisson, Madame Loreal recalls how, after the blast had swept over them, they fled in panic – not to meet again for more than two years.

The explosion

Down in the area of the Avant Port, the blast, so long expected, still came as a huge shock to the clusters of prisoners either waiting under guard on the quaysides or landing from German ships. In one shocking instant they had been transformed, in their captors' eyes, from the defeated remnants of a force whose losses were entirely out of proportion to the damage they had caused, into dangerous and unpredictable desperadoes who had sown who knows what terror in the buildings and waters around them. Beattie was in a dockside office having the futility of attempting simply to ram the massive caisson pointed out to him, at the very moment when the thunder of exploding Amatol tore the caisson from its seat and

folded it back against the dry dock wall. The hopeful évadées, still hiding in drain and cellar, took heart from the aural evidence of success in spite of the fact that, by putting the Germans even more on their guard, it might well impact negatively on their attempts to escape. Everywhere attitudes changed, the mantle of victor slipping from German shoulders onto British ones – a reversal of roles which hardened attitudes towards both POWs and civilians alike.

Out in La Baule, where Watson had been 'overjoyed to meet Johnny Roderick and Hoppy [Hopwood] again,' news of *Campbeltown's* belated eruption came in the form of loud shouting, which woke him from an exhausted sleep to find 'their' Germans had exploded too.

A small German petty officer was positively screaming with rage...telling us at the top of his voice that we were all going to be shot, and indeed the guards looked angry enough to do it there and then. We infuriated them further by our indifference to their threats. They did not appreciate that we were so physically and emotionally drained that being put up against a wall or shot where we lay was a matter of resignation rather than fear. In the

The remains of *Campbeltown* lie in 'Normandie' Dock. HARRY JAMES

event everything slowly calmed down.

(Dr W H Watson, MBE.,MC: unpublished narrative)

Watson's account links this reaction to the realisation on the part of the Germans that they had made a grave, and uncharacteristic, error in assuming,

> *that the British would have gone to all that trouble just to scuttle an old destroyer which could be dragged off or broken up. The explosive was well concealed but the search party could have been more imaginative. It must have made then even angrier to realise that they only had themselves to blame. They should have assumed that the* Campbeltown *was a Trojan Horse.*

(Dr W H Watson, MBE.,MC: unpublished narrative)

Added to this was the fact that, directly as a consequence of their lack of thoroughness, the explosion had exacted a cost in lives which ran into the hundreds, this, tragically, including a number of women who had come to the area with their uniformed escorts. The various experts having, earlier that morning, inspected the ship and declared it safe, the burned and battered relic had quickly become 'the place to be seen', a magnet for the curious of all ranks who came from near and far to impress and to be impressed, and whose bodies were all but atomized in a single, shattering moment of time. The scale of the destruction was

174

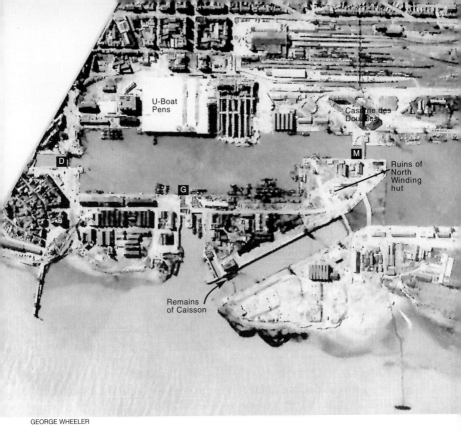

U-Boat Pens

Caserne des Douanes

D

M

Ruins of North Winding hut

G

Remains of Caisson

GEORGE WHEELER

The 'Normandie' Dock, looking toward the northern caisson. Portions of *Campbeltown* **remain long after the raid.** COLLECTION : ECOMUSEE DE SAINT-NAZAIRE

later recalled by an eye-witness, a French electrical mechanic who, on passing through the area on Monday en-route to his place of work at Ressort 8, noticed how dazed and bewildered the German troops still seemed to be. He was able to see that the caisson had been destroyed: however, the most visible, and shocking, evidence of *Campbeltown's* explosion was a litter of human remains so extensive that working parties had not yet succeeded in shovelling everything up.

In thrusting the caisson off its seat, the blast, which had torn *Campbeltown* apart from her forepeak right back to her midsection, had exposed the dock to the Loire whose waters flooded in, carrying the remains of the destroyer forward and ripping *Schlettstadt* and *Passat* from their moorings. Although damaged by charges placed earlier by the parties of Brett and Burtinshaw, the inner caisson held, preventing the even greater disaster of having the whole Penhoët Basin opened to the sea. Taken in conjunction with the destruction of the winding houses and Pumping Station, *Campbeltown's* immolation had effectively sealed the fate of this one great facility which, had the Germans even bothered to try, would have taken at least a year and a half to repair. As it was, the evolution of German naval strategy saw all her major surface ships transferred to home waters, the collapse of the *Kriegsmarine's* Atlantic dream removing all priority from the enormous effort involved. Once home to the mightiest of ships, the 'Normandie' dock was sealed off so as to restore the operational integrity of the Penhoët Basin. Left to moulder, it would remain, for Occupied and Occupier alike, an ever-present reminder that men of courage and determination had come once to Saint-Nazaire – and would surely come again.

The 'Normandie' Dock, looking towards the Loire estuary. The caisson destroyed by *Campbeltown* has been replaced by a dam. MRS M. ASHCROFT

Chapter Twelve

THREADS

In an effort to regain control of a situation already exacerbated by the disproportionate loss of officers on and around the apparently harmless destroyer, the process was speeded up by means of which the POWs were moved along the chain, from Saint-Nazaire to La Baule to their first holding camps in Rennes. With the soldiers and sailors gone the local population would be deprived of images likely to provoke sedition, creating an environment within which the garrison could undertake repairs, search for other 'infernal' devices left behind by the raiders, and begin the process of apportioning blame for the catalogue of errors which had brought them to their present pass.

Having spent only a handful of hours in La Baule, where their numbers had been steadily augmented by new arrivals full of the news of their success, the able-bodied were again, as described by Copland;

herded into trucks, backs to the guards – very unpleasant Military Police – and we set off upon a nightmare drive of some 7 hours to Rennes. Our driver seemed to take all his corners on two wheels so that, what with being shaken to pieces, cramped to death and snarled at by our unpleasant warders, it seemed sweet relief when we entered our first Prisoner of War Camp.

We climbed stifly from our trucks and to our astonishment found ourselves almost surrounded by French coloured troops, prisoners also, laughing, shouting and throwing cigarettes to us. All attempts by the Germans to prevent this welcome and the kindly generosity accompanying it were in vain. Rifle butts raised in threat had but a temporary effect... . I shall not ever forget that welcome.

(Major W O Copland, DSO: unpublished narrative)

The Hermitage in sunnier times. The CHARIOT wounded were cared for in a makeshift ward, immediately after the raid, on the ground floor to the right of the main entrance.

For the wounded, spread about the floor of their 'luxury' accommodation in L'Hermitage, the drive to Rennes would have been a stroll in the park when compared to the pain and discomfort

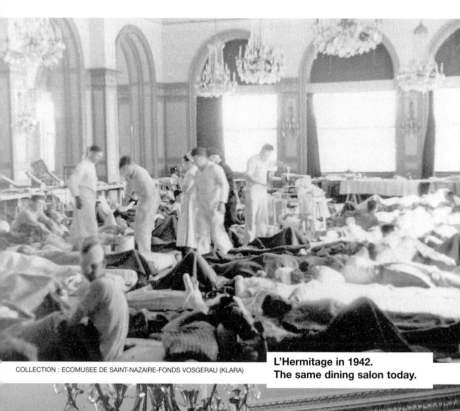

COLLECTION : ECOMUSEE DE SAINT-NAZAIRE-FONDS VOSGERAU (KLARA)

**L'Hermitage in 1942.
The same dining salon today.**

awaiting them. Corran Purdon's memory is of being,

forced to put on hospital nightshirts and lie on mattresses, closely packed on the ground while German sailors, Tommy guns at the alert, moved around, covering us as we lay there. I had Micky Wynn on one side of me. Although he had lost an eye he was typically brave and cheerful. On my other side was Sergeant Dick Bradley, MM, shot through the body, but also cheerful and gallant. It was the most depressing time of my life; the realisation that we were prisoners of war, that we would not be quickly rejoining our loved ones and friends, coupled with the squalour of our condition and the unpleasantness of our captors, came in massive contrast to the excitement and elation of the operation.

We did what we could to help our severely injured and to keep up our spirits. The behaviour of some of the Nazi medical orderlies and staff, women as well as men, was callous and unpleasant and certainly induced a feeling of hatred that many of us had not entertained up to then. I still recall the moronic naval youth who, when I was injected, presumably with anti-tetanus, threw the hypodermic syringe at my buttock like a dart, and I still remember feeling the point of its needle against the bone.

(Major General C W B Purdon, CBE.,MC.,CPM:
List the Bugle p39)

With the German wounded being seen-to first, it was late in the day before the prisoners were introduced to the horrors of operations either without anaesthetics or where such palliatives were ineffective. Stuart Chant was carried to a room in which kitchen tables, pressed into medical service, were surrounded by stretchers lying about the floor. Placed on one of the tables, ether was applied, which promised only to deceive - for it failed to take effect, the removal of shrapnel and ball from Chant's right arm, left leg and right knee, proving to be a period of 'unmitigated horror and pain'. When Watson's turn came, attempts were made to manipulate his shattered arm into a position where a splint could be applied, by an orderly who,

was obviously trying to be gentle, but his tentative manipulations only served to increase the pain. When he saw this he became quite rattled. All the time he was muttering to me in German and it was easy to understand that he was apologising. Poor man! The sweat stood out on his face as well as mine, and he was ashen. I do not know who was suffering the most.

(Dr W H Watson, MBE.,MC: unpublished narrative)

179

Within Saint-Nazaire, during the dragging, anguished hours of Saturday afternoon, life was lived in hushed tones as the readjustment was made from the excitement and terror of the night before, to the disheartening realisation that, with the 'Tommies' gone, renewed German suspicion of French motives and intent was only likely to make their own lives even more difficult than before. The search for enemy soldiers, weapons, and the tools and agents of sabotage continued with a new and sometimes brutal intensity, born of the desire for revenge and the fear that other blasts might follow.

In light of the restrictions placed on movement by the Germans' almost total domination of port, town and surrounding countryside, it is all the more remarkable that some of the hopeful évadées not only survived through the whole of Saturday, but even succeeded in breaking through the supposedly watertight 'cordon sanitaire'. George Wheeler's account of his own and Lance Corporal Sims' experiences, describes how:

> When we left our hiding place about midnight we discovered that we had been lying under the house next door to the German Kommandantur. We made our way through the streets of the new town and cut across country, arriving at a village which was l'immaculée. We had no maps, but it was a fairly moonlit night. We hid in a haystack in which a hole had been cut to form an air-raid shelter. We remained there until about 1900hrs (29 Mar), when a friend of the farmer came for hay and discovered us. He yelled "Camarade" and we yelled "Camarade" in return. After I had asked for food and explained who we were, the man brought us food and wine, and about 2300 hrs he took us to the farm house and fitted us out with civilian clothes and gave us 250 francs each. He also advised us to get rid of traces of our identity, to keep to the small roads, and to make for Nantes. We gave him our Colts, which he said he "might be using one day".

(Corporal G R Wheeler, MM: after action report)

For the Haines group in their cellar, hopes of escape were complicated by wounds. To give everyone the best possible chance Haines split the party into three pairs, each of which would choose its own course through the darkened streets above. Haines and Lance Sergeant Challington made it out of the cellar successfully, as did Lance Corporal Douglas and Private Harding: however, when the time for action arrived, his incapacitating wounds prevented Corporal Bob Wright from accompanying the Guardsman, Lance Corporal Howarth, himself lightly wounded. Douglas and Harding made it out of town, and would eventually succeed in returning to Britain, via Marseilles.

Howarth had the good fortune to meet, and be looked after by, the Baratte family, before undertaking his own perilous odyssey southwards, returning to Britain in October. Haines and Challington almost made it into the open countryside before being caught. Left to his own devices, Bob Wright did attempt a passage of the hostile streets: but he too was taken, his wounds ensuring a speedy passage to the doubtful comforts of L'Hermitage.

Of the eight Commandos who had tried for home, George Wheeler was to earn the distinction of being first to return, arriving in Britain on 21 May after he and Sims had crossed the Pyrenees to Gibraltar. Considering all the trials and tribulations the two had managed to overcome, George recalls that, rather than being received with open arms, 'when I came back to Plymouth I was regarded with great suspicion. They thought I was a plant.'

On Sunday 29 March, Hitler's headquarters became more a source of stress than the the port itself. The Führer was very angry indeed to learn that so heavily defended a base could have been penetrated so easily, and ordered the C-in-C West to determine what went wrong. He also wished to know if it was proposed to court-martial the senior officer responsible.

Having conducted an enquiry, Field Marshal Von Rundstedt concluded that no single officer could be held responsible, and that all concerned had done their best in the circumstances. Wholly dissatisfied with what he saw as a 'whitewash', Hitler pursued the matter further, but his antagonism served only to cause a rift between Party and Navy, prompting Grand Admiral Raeder to write to Keitel

Looking across the South Entrance towards the Rue du Port.
COLLECTION : ECOMUSEE DE SAINT-NAZAIRE-FONDS WIEDENHOFER

demanding both an explanation of this interference in Naval affairs, and an apology. With Saint-Nazaire being such an important U-Boat base, arrangements were put in place immediately to enhance defence: but no heads rolled.

For those waiting at home for really accurate information upon which to base an assessment of the raid's success, Palm Sunday also marked the return to British shores of Ryder and the remants of his fleet.

Having, by 1700 the previous day, put sufficient distance between themselves and the hostile shore, ML160, ML307 and ML443 had turned north, sailed on through the night and sighted the Lizard at 1000 hrs. By noon Sunday they were entering Falmouth harbour, their return a quiet, introspective, emotional affair. ML443 was first to tie up at Prince of Wales Pier. During the fraught run home, her command structure had changed yet again, with the rescued Platt resuming his captaincy in place of Horlock. The 443 was followed in by Boyd's 160 and Wallis' ML307, and the process began of transferring the wounded into waiting ambulances. This done, the boats' remaining Commandos were returned to the 'PJC', their numbers contrasting starkly with memories of the boisterous company who had given her such life only a handful of days before.

Also putting into Falmouth harbour were the destroyers *Cleveland* and *Brocklesby*, Commander Sayer having decided to split his force late on Saturday so that a search might be carried out for the 'lost' MLs without prejudicing the needs of the wounded on board *Tynedale* and *Atherstone*. His search having proved fruitless, Sayer brought his two ships into port in the afternoon, at which point the body of gunner Savage was ferried ashore from *Brocklesby* to be prepared for burial.

With some of the wounded requiring immediate treatment, *Tynedale* and *Atherstone* had been ordered to make directly for Plymouth where they, too, arrived on Sunday. As a priority the wounded were transferred to the Royal Naval Hospital at Stonehouse, while the remaining Commando survivors were put up in Seaton Barracks prior to returning to Scotland, where the process could begin of rebuilding 2 Commando. For Ryder, the occasion was heavy with emotion, his account describing how:

> We eventually berthed alongside in Devonport dockyard and were seeing to the discharge of our wounded. I remember standing on the jetty watching the scene and wondering what the reaction would be to all this. I was conscious – very conscious – that we had failed to re-embark our comrades-in-arms and had left them to their fate. I felt personally responsible for the decision to leave without them. I was in an exhausted

condition with all that had happened. We believed that we had blown up the lock and I felt elated at having struck a blow.

At that moment a Wren despatch rider, braking hard, drew up alongside of me - "Commander Ryder?". She handed me a buff envelope which I tore open. This, referring to previous correspondence, was to confirm that I had incurred their Lordships' displeasure for not having exercised collision stations in my previous vessel. It seemed rather inconsequential at that moment.

(Captain R E D Ryder, VC.,RN: unpublished narrative)

Exhausted though he might have been, Ryder was denied rest by the myriad urgent demands and responsibilities awaiting him on shore. Almost immediately he had to travel up to London to report in person to Mountbatten, Admiral Pound the First Sea Lord, and others. Then there were casualty and action reports, letters to next of kin and recommendations for awards. Perhaps most arduous of all was a press conference, in London, organized by the Ministry of Information. Faced by several hundred reporters, while bound by the need to maintain secrecy, Ryder, who was most anxious to pay tribute to Sam Beattie, fell foul of an MOI official who declared that it was against regulations to mention names. Not in the mood to be told what to do by petty officials, Ryder's uncompromising reply was to the effect that:

I was appointed Force Commander. As far as I am aware I have not yet been relieved of this responsibility so as Force Commander I would like to make it clear that you Ladies and Gentlemen have my permission to publish Commander Beattie's name. This was very warmly recieved, except of course by the poor MOI official whom I had snubbed. There was no come back.

(Captain R E D Ryder, VC.,RN: unpublished narrative)

In Falmouth, Monday March 30th saw the final laying to rest of the body of Able Seaman William Savage, who was interred in Madeira Road Cemetery beside Leading Motor Mechanic Tom Parker who,

Kriegsmarine in the streets of the Old Town following the raid.

severely wounded on board ML447, had been rescued only to die on board ML160, almost within sight of home.

In Saint-Nazaire too, Monday began as a day of reflection, of gathering together the threads of lives disrupted both by the violence of the raid itself, and by the Germans' harsh response to it. Quietly, tentatively, civilians took to the streets again and workers returned to the docks with their macabre reminders of the human toll exacted by *Campbeltown's* explosion. The streets, alleys, bridges and locks which just forty-eight hours before had echoed to reports of gunfire, the concussion of grenades and the cries of men in extremis, still seemed to buzz with the excitement of seeing the occupiers humbled: yet great care had to be taken not to antagonize by word or deed soldiers and sailors stung by fear, embittered by losses and now deeply suspicious of treachery amongst those over whom they once believed they had complete control. Superficially at least there may have been an air of returning normality: but it was a chimera, as Wynn's torpedoes were shortly to prove, having lain dormant to the point where their damage would now prove as shattering to fragile morale as to the fabric of their intended target, the Old Entrance lock.

The unreliability of delayed-action fuzes was such that Wynn's torpedoes did not go up until Monday afternoon, the first missile erupting at 1600 and carrying with it the outer lock gate. For the already strained garrison this could only be interpreted as sabotage, which meant that a collective anger, sometimes bordering on panic, was immediately directed towards the entirely blameless civilian population. Had there been any doubts about French complicity, these were swept away within the hour by the explosion of the second torpedo, its concussion finally snapping nerves already stretched to breaking point.

For the Germans, the Old Town, with its closely packed buildings and narrow streets, was seen as an ideal hiding place for 'terrorists' and saboteurs. Accordingly it was evacuated, with families ejected from their homes and incarcerated in the distant Sud 1 bunker, where a fraught night was passed without food, water – even light.

Many of their officers having been lost in the destroyer's explosion, the reaction of German troops was unpredictable, on occasions degenerating into indiscriminate 'firefights', with imagined adversaries, whose casualties included civilians, members of their own forces – even Organisation Todt workers, whose uniforms in the heat of the moment were taken for British khaki. The area of the docks, to which workers had only just returned, began to clear again, as men in fear for their own and their families' lives, made for the bridges that would carry them back towards the body of the town.

The effect of all these movements, whether generated by panic or carried out at the point of a gun, was to clear that whole portion of Saint-Nazaire which lay east of the South Entrance and the two great basins. Into this vacuum moved parties of troops whose crude attempts to purge the area of its malign content, real or imagined, were only the first step in a process which would see almost all of the Old Town razed to the ground. Today, on the rise once occupied by this ancient construction, there is nothing to be seen of the tenements mentioned in contemporary accounts: yet, just as would be the case with the primary fortifications, a number of structures still remain which, as well as being closely related to the raid, were sufficiently important to the Germans to be spared the general destruction. Immediately to the east of what was then Bridge 'B', lies the Power Station complex; and right next to it is the 'Santé Maritime' building - more properly the Service de Sanitaire Maritime - the cellar of which had, on the night of the raid, housed Dr Edmond Bizard's aid post.

Having been so unceremoniously ejected from their homes, the population of Old Saint-Nazaire was moved out of town on Tuesday morning, to temporary accommodation in a camp on Savenay racecourse. Later in the week they would be permitted to return to their homes – but only to collect what remained of their possessions before the process of destruction got under way.

During this term of trial for the people of Saint-Nazaire, who had been warned that further aggression would result in the taking of hostages, the wounded raiders continued to receive treatment in La Baule. Perhaps because of their 'vulnerable' condition, attempts were made to elicit information which could then be used to bolster German propagana claims of British failure. At one point, a group of civilians arrived, who purported to be members of the Swiss Red Cross: however, as 'Tiger' Watson recalls, they were not quite all that they appeared to be.

This deputation had a cumbersome recording machine and declared that as it would take a very long time for our relatives to hear that we were alive through official channels, we could record a short message "for our loved ones" that could be broadcast. They had prevailed upon one or two of the more serious cases to speak before some alert chap demanded to see their credentials. After a brief attempt to brazen it out, the group hastily decamped pursued by our jeers and catcalls.

We soon learnt who those spurious Swiss really were. One evening, shortly after the Germans switched on the radio, the hateful sneering voice of "Lord Haw Haw" ...filled the room.

After mocking the pathetic total failure of the attempt on Saint-Nazaire, he went on: "And here are the voices of some of your relatives. Some of the survivors now in our hands".

(Dr W H Watson, MBE, MC: unpublished narrative)

As a member of the 'walking wounded' who could speak French well, Corran Purdon was one of a small group;

taken away to identify a number of our dead comrades. They were already in open coffins, between twenty and thirty of them, and it was a terribly sad and unpleasant task. I remember the body of the superb fighting NCO, Sergeant Tom Durrant, VC, and all the wounds he had suffered in his brave and self-sacrificial final battle.'

(Major General C W B Purdon, CBE.,MC.,CPM:
List the Bugle pp 40-1)

On the Wednesday following the raid, Corran was one of a larger group of officers and men ferried a short distance to take part in a ceremony during which the dead were interred in what is now the intensely moving Escoublac-la-Baule War Cemetery. His account describes how:

Those of us who could walk were given back our clothes in order to attend the funeral of our fallen comrades. The Germans were correct and punctilious and obviously wanted to honour our brave men. It was a dreadfully depressing occasion. I was one of four who lowered coffins into the grave and I remember

The Germans saw to it that those killed in the raid received full military honours. MAJOR GENERAL CORRAN PURDON

gripping the rope like one possessed as I felt it, slimy with wet
mud, slipping in my hand, and the feeling of relief when the act
of lowering was successfully completed. We passed in single file
by a Union Flag draped coffin, paying our last respects with an
Eyes Right.

(Major General C W B Purdon, CBE.,MC.,CPM:
List the Bugle p40)

After about a week in L'Hermitage, the wounded were also moved
away to Rennes, this time to St Vincent's Hospital, where treatment
continued for many. Transport for the stretcher cases involved a
hellishly uncomfortable journey by hospital train. Arthur Ashcroft was
greatly moved by the attention paid to Tommy McCormack who,
unable to feed himself, was tended by a German doctor who sat on his
bunk and fed the badly wounded soldier with a spoon. McCormack's
life was destined to end in Rennes, where he lies today, one of the 169
soldiers and sailors to lose their lives on the raid, out of the 611 who
took part, a fatal casualty rate of more than one in four.

Particularly for units so closely knit as the Commandos, who had
lived and trained together over months and years to the point where
some of the Troops had, in effect, become extended 'families', such
losses were especially galling. Micky Burn recalls a lengthy period of
waiting for news of his own 6 Troop, during which time uncertainty
kept his hopes alive. Eventually, however,

a time came when I could pretend to myself no longer. Until
then it had been as if I had been going over and over that night's
events in front of a blurred screen with sound commentary off.
Hope had muted them, confusing what in my heart I knew to be
the truth. Now it came on full blast. The guns came on, the
explosions, the cries from the boats, the burning oil and the
hideous nature of their deaths. Night passed, the sun rose for a
moment over the Loire like a Viking funeral pyre. And then all
grandeur died, river and sky turned grey, the beach was strewn
with bodies of dead men and burnt-out ships, and I knew that all
those I had waited for had been killed.

(Michael Burn, MC: *Turned Towards the Sun*, pp 143-4)

To this stark accounting of the fallen must be added the 200 or so
young men, many of them wounded, who, after initial confinement in
La Baule and Rennes, would eventually be distributed to POW camps
throughout the Reich. In time these camps would come to include the
notorious Stalag V111B, at Lamsdorf, Oflag 1X A/H Spangenberg, and
the supposedly escape-proof – though not to Lieutenant Commander
Billie Stephens – Oflag 1V C, Colditz. Initially, however, all were

Oflag IX A/H Spangenberg, 1942/3 showing guard hut and drawbridge.
LT COLONEL IAN CHANT SEMPILL

After the war this was all that remained of the area west of the U-Boat pens. The pale structure mid image was a command bunker constructed later in the war. COLLECTION : ECOMUSEE DE SAINT-NAZAIRE/ARCHIVES MUNICIPALES DE SAINT-NAZAIRE

NAVAL OFFICER POWs: MARLAG UND MILAG NORD.

Rear row, left to right: Lieutenant Bill Tillie, Mid, CO of ML 268; Sub Lieutenant Sam Haighton, RNVR, ML 192; Warrant Engineer W H Locke, RN, DSC, HMS *Campbeltown;* Sub Lieutenant Bob Nock, RNVR, DSC, CO of ML 298; unknown; Sub Lieutenant Philip Dark, RNVR, ML 306; unknown.

Front row, left to right: Sub Lieutenant W Pirie-Mewes, RNVR, ML 267; Lieutenant Ted Burt, RNVR, DSC, CO of ML262; Lieutenant Commander Sam Beattie, VC, RN, Captain of HMS *Campbeltown;* Sub Lieutenant W J Heaven, RNVR, ML 177; Sub Lieutenant Pat Landy, RANVR, ML 306; Sub Lieutenant G E A Barham, RNVR, ML457; Sub Lieutenant Robbie Roberts, RNVR, ML 262. E.C.A. ROBERTS, N.R. NOCK

NAVAL RATING POWS: MARLAG UND MILAG NORD.

Rear row, left to right: Leading Telegraphist Jim Laurie, RN, ML 192; Chief Motor Mechanic J G 'Geordie' Welch, RN, ML 457; Leading Seaman J H 'Jimmy' Gleeson, RN, ML 267; Leading Seaman Sam Rivett, RN, DSM, Mid, ML 268; Chief Motor Mechanic Bill Lovegrove, CGM, MTB 74.

Middle row, left to right: Telegraphist R H Newman RNZN, ML306; Motor Mechanic Christopher 'Kit' Aston, RN, ML 192; Leading Seaman Bill Leaney, RN, Mid, ML 262; Petty Officer Motor Mechanic John Rafferty, RN ML 177; Ordnance Artificer Frank Wherrell, RN, HMS *Campbeltown;* Stoker Petty Officer Archie Pitt, RN, HMS *Campbeltown.*

Front row, left to right: A/Petty Officer Hugh McPhail 'Jock' Bruce, RN, ML192; Leading Motor Mechanic Hugh Irvine, RN, ML177; Leading Motor Mechanic Jack Pryde, RN, ML 262; Petty Officer R Hambley, RN, DSM ML 298; Petty Officer Bill Stocker, RN, HMS *Campbeltown;* Leading Seaman John Castle, RN, ML 268.

brought together in Marlag und Milag Nord, a camp for naval and merchant navy detainees situated north east of Bremen, near Westertimke.

Charles Newman was later to write of the men, that,

It is needless to say that they fought like we knew they would fight, they took the news that there was no re-embarkation with a laugh, and they have carried themselves with dignity all through their...years of prisoner-of-wardom, never shown any down in the mouth or despondent ways and have continued and I hope always will continue to be part of a very happy family.

(Lieutenant Colonel A C Newman, VC: unpublished narrative)

Essentially that 'family' was born at Westertimke, where, for a time, officers and men, soldiers and sailors alike, remained together, their unified presence only serving to make firmer still the links already forged in the heat of battle. In post-war years the family was to take the form of a Society whose primary aims would be, in Newman's words, to maintain friendships 'of the kind which should not be allowed to drift apart', to foster a close and supportive relationship with the people of Saint-Nazaire, who suffered 'to a very great extent in the nature of reprisals [and] did all they possibly could to join in and help', and to accept as a duty that they 'should never, and must never, forget those of their comrades who gave their lives...'

The first 'official' meeting of the Saint Nazaire Society took place in 1946 and was attended by two hundred soldiers and sailors. While rather fewer veterans now remain, the Society which was Newman's dream is very much alive, still actively supporting the principles first enunciated by him in the shadow of war.

Given all the years that have passed since he and Ryder and Beattie sailed their imperilled fleet into the estuary of the Loire, surely there can be no greater tribute to the achievements of all the 'Charioteers' than that they are remembered still by a new and ever-expanding family of those who honour and appreciate the courage that keeps us free.

EPILOGUE

During the years which followed CHARIOT, the construction of Hitler's *Atlantikwall* saw the defences of Saint-Nazaire and its hinterland increase markedly in both scale and complexity. Intensified Allied air activity saw a steady augmentation of Flak defences; work was begun on providing the U-Boat pens with additional overhead protection; and coastal emplacements were more heavily fortified, many being fitted with even larger calibre cannon.

Following the successful Allied invasion of June, 1944, German forces trapped within Brittany fell back on that region's U-Boat bases, taking advantage of their deep defences while, at the same time, ensuring the continued functioning of the U-Flotillas based therein. Eventually classed as fortresses to be held to the bitter end, these enemy 'pockets' were invested by a succession of American units beginning, in the case of Saint-Nazaire, with the 83rd Infantry Division, who were relieved shortly thereafter by the 94th Infantry Division. Charged primarily with containing the 30,000 assorted troops of *'Festungkommandant' Generalleutnant* Hans Junck, the 94th remained in place until December 1944, at which point Major General Herman F Kramer's 66th 'Black Panther' Division took over, supported by Free French units led by Lieutenant General Raymond Chomel.

In spite of the liberation of most of the rest of France, the civilians who remained within the 'Poche de Saint-Nazaire' continued to suffer the hardship and ignominy of occupation until the very last days of the war, Junck refusing to surrender until 8 May, 1945, the formal ceremony of capitulation taking place just three days after that. The port was free at last – although after five long years of war the tide of returning inhabitants was met by little more than a ghost-town, its heart a bleak and dispiriting sea of rubble.

One of the many preparing to meet the grim challenge of reconstruction was Fred Caldecott, an Englishman who had long ago left Liverpool to work in the shipyards beside the Loire – a 'foreigner' who had married, settled and adopted the town as his own. His thoughts and the thoughts of other Nazairiens are summed up by Alan Burgess in a moving article entitled 'My Town is St. Nazaire', published by Radio Times on 29 April, 1949. The following extract, quoted with the kind permission of Radio Times, captures perfectly both the spirit of the time and the particular regard in which the 'Charioteers' were held by men and women who, in all too many cases, had lost everything to the years of conflict.

When the war ended most of St. Nazaire's forty-five thousand inhabitants had left the town. It was a place of ruin, of rubble, of skeleton houses. Only one colossal building remained, the German submarine pen. The docks, the foundries, the great shipbuilding yard of Chantier Penhoët were smashed – so it seemed – beyond repair.

But the men of St. Nazaire came back from the wars, back from the outer perimeter of the town, back from the outlying seaside districts of Pornichet, and La Baule, from the farmhouse, the barn, hut, prison and concentration camp, to start again. Houses? Who wanted houses? Priorities were for new ships on the stocks, ships being refitted, ships being repaired. Bring back prosperity to the shipyards... and prosperity would return to the town.

Even today, as a town, St. Nazaire hardly exists. Two thousand "prefabs" stand on cleared ground. There is a tiny town centre of prefabricated shops.

But the shipyards roar and rattle with activity: liners in the process of being refitted, cargo boats waiting for their trials, a thirty-thousand-ton oil tanker – largest in the world – just laid on the stocks. And in the huge graving dock – unforgettable to a number of heroic young men who blew its gate sky high on a certain dark night in 1942 – now lies the ex-German liner Europa, taken by the French as a war reparation, and renamed with much justification – Liberté. It rises high above the town, a resurgent symbol of activity and reconstruction.

Of that eventful night in 1942, the people of St. Nazaire have many memories. It was while we were recording in an iron foundry that we met some of the French workers who had helped the British invaders on "the night of the Commando". Into the manager's office came a succession of middle-aged French workmen dressed in blue dungarees and twisting black berets in nervous fingers, to show us faded British identity discs given as mementos, to tell how they acted as guides, how they fought, and how, after the raid, they helped some of our soldiers to escape. The penalty for this sort of escapade was death by a German firing squad, yet these French workers were concerned only in telling us about the courage of the British.

It is difficult to explain how moving these short interviews were. But it is certain that the men of the Royal Navy and the Commandos who came up the Loire that night left a mark in the imagination of the people of St. Nazaire which will not easily be erased.

193

APPENDIX 1

TOURING THE SAINT-NAZAIRE BATTLEFIELD

(approx: 4km – 2.5 miles)

Given the degree to which Allied bombing all but destroyed the commercial and residential heart of 1940s Saint-Nazaire, it is all the more remarkable that the general form of the CHARIOT battlefield has survived six decades of reconstruction and expansion virtually unchanged. The new town retains little that would be recognized by Newman or Ryder; while, east and north of what had then been the fuel oil storage area, reclamation has significantly increased that area of the Loire shore dedicated to the shipbuilding and aircraft industries. And yet, sandwiched between these major zones of development, the twin 'islands' which Newman and his men had fought so hard to isolate retain their integrity still, cosmetic changes to the buildings they support having left largely unchanged the locks, docks, bridges and key structures only too familiar to the planners of 1942. The 'Normandie' dock, with its rebuilt caissons, and pumping and winding houses, remains a hugely valuable asset, its vast proportions as often

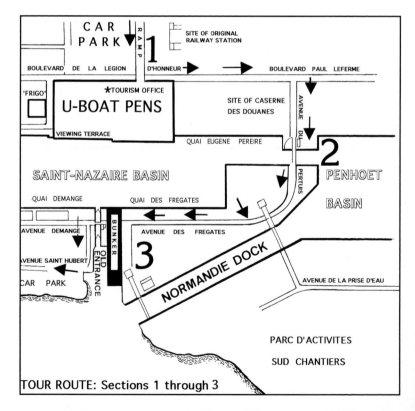

as not home to liners and cruise-ships being refitted; the Old Mole wants only blockhouses to regain its wartime menace; and the South Entrance is still that same tranquil stretch of water by means of which well-provisioned U-Boats once entered the Atlantic, and rust-stained veterans of the convoy battles brought home their weary crews.

Neatly splitting the eastern quays of the Saint-Nazaire Basin, the original Old Entrance, with the gates restored which once fell foul of Wynn's torpedoes, is now dwarfed by the massive reinforced concrete bunker which rendered bomb-and raid-proof a parallel lock constructed in the aftermath of CHARIOT to guarantee free access to the basin: while directly opposite and taking up much of the basin's western extent, the formidable, brooding mass of the U-Boat complex now glowers over scenes of peace and colour, its uniform greyness adding to the impression of a structure still sulking over the loss of its wartime dignity and purpose.

Modern attempts to rescue both of these massive structures have resulted in the apt conversion of the Old Entrance bunker into a long-term home for the decommissioned French submarine *Espadon*, and the development of the once almost derelict pens into an attraction central to the city's burgeoning tourist economy. Each has undeniable visual impact; however, their accessibility, modern facilities and immense historical significance make the strategically located pens the ideal starting point from which to tour the battlefield they still so completely dominate.

1: THE U-BOAT PENS

Occupying almost 300m of quayside frontage this complex structure, with its gun towers, firing embrasures and fourteen dark chamber frontages, will be as much a companion to the visitor today as it was an ever-present menace for the raiders of 1942. Reaching 18m high and stretching 124m back towards the Boulevard de la Légion d'Honneur, it could accommodate a total of twenty boats along with all their support, repair and maintenance facilities. Although the numbers which once surmounted each chamber entrance have long since fallen foul of time, they would, when the structure was complete, have run from north to south, identifying pens 1 through 8 as dry docks (some still under construction in March of 1942), and 9 A-B to 14 A-B as 'wet' pens each capable of housing two boats side by side. Intended right from the start to be a fortress in its own right – a claim which no one will dispute who takes the time to explore its interior and marvel at its humbling proportions – the whole was an impregnable enemy strongpoint whose malign influence, right at the very heart of CHARIOT, cannot be over-emphasized.

In recognition of the fact that their physical domination of the port remains undiminished by time, the pens are now home to Saint-Nazaire's main Tourist Information Office, the interests of the public being served by exhibitions, a well-equipped gift shop, a cafe/bar and washrooms. With a number of the inner walls on the west side having been removed, there is open access to the middle tranche of pens from the large car park on the other side of the Boulevard: indeed some of the pens can be walked along their full length to the basin frontage overlooking the Old Entrance, the Quai Demange and the Quai des Frégates. Within the echoing chambers, and especially in the area occupied by the multi-storeyed service bays which once ran alongside the railway giving access to the rear of each pen, the process of cutting through internal walls betrays thicknesses approaching 3 metres, the sheer scale of construction manifesting in concrete the Nazi dream of securing the Reich for 'a thousand years'.

Central to the process of understanding fully the role the structure played in CHARIOT, is an exploration of its 'bombproof' roof, whose strength and elevation were such an advantage to German riflemen and machine-gunners. Rising gently from the car park west of the Boulevard, a broad ramp gives easy access to the amazing complex of reinforced concrete beams, slabs and blast chambers which were designed to break up and render ineffective even the largest bombs in the Allied arsenal. Combining into a system known as Fangrost, it consists of head-high lateral supports upon which were laid closely-packed beams in the shape of an inverted 'U'. Although never fully realized – it is complete over pens 1 through 5 and partially complete over its middle third, the southernmost portion reflecting the look of the structure prior to reinforcement – the system survived the war largely undamaged, its mass at least partially explaining how the whole pen complex managed to consume almost half a million cubic metres of concrete.

The roof over the U-Boat Pens, looking north-west over the completed portion of the *Fangrost* bomb-proofing system.

Within certain limits it is now possible to walk through the blast chambers towards the basin frontage, always provided adequate notice is taken of the low headroom and the impenetrability of the beams overhead. Following the marked route leads to the tall gun tower which stands directly above the entrance to pen 8 and can be accessed by steep steps. Constructed to house a quadruple 20mm cannon, it surmounts a covered firing gallery which extends along the entire seaward face of the structure, its roof, between pens 8 and 14, forming a broad *Terrasse Panoramique*. Although neither tower nor gallery existed at the time of CHARIOT, their unparalleled view of the dockyard demonstrates just how vulnerable Newman's isolated parties really were; for the advantage enjoyed by defenders concealed at such a height is obvious, their physical domination allowing them to bring the greater part of the Commando operating area under direct aimed fire. Given such extreme exposure it is all the more impossible to conceive of how so few raiders, challenged so directly, managed to achieve so much.

On leaving the pens for Bridge 'M', the surrounding scene, so redolent of change and modernity, speaks volumes for the almost total failure of the wartime Allied air assaults. Of the 20,000 tons of bombs released over the Biscay ports, little was achieved beyond the destruction of French civilian lives and property. The campaign cost 100 bombers, and claimed 500 lives within Saint-Nazaire alone, in return for which not a single U-Boat was hit, nor were their operations disrupted in any way, and nor were their crews at any time endangered as the precaution had already been taken of billeting these well outside the danger area. As a consequence of the destruction one of the few original buildings visible as one moves to the right along the Boulevard de la Légion d'Honneur, is the façade of the original railway station as it was before the complex of rails and sidings was moved to its present position at the northern end of the Avenue de la République. The façade is directly in line with the powerful annexe running alongside pen 1. As the last part of the U-Boat complex to be completed, during 1943, its great strength more than compensated for its exposed position. Controlling the north and west approaches at the point where the service railway once entered the interior through strong steel doors, its concrete face is chillingly punctuated by armoured embrasures for both anti-tank and machine-guns.

2: BRIDGE 'M' AND THE 'NORMANDIE' DOCK, NORTH CAISSON

On clearing the concrete mass of the pens, the Boulevard de la Légion d'Honneur becomes the Boulevard Paul Leferme, a thoroughfare once bounded to the west by the broad swathe of the railway yards. Approaching the point at which the Avenue du Pertuis joins the Boulevard, a footbridge used to cross the multiplicity of tracks, joining the Boulevard with the Rue Henri Gautier. This was the escape route for which confused and frightened dockyard workers and O.T. personnel were making following the delayed explosion of Wynn's torpedoes, when fired upon by panicked defenders.

While over the course of the war, this general area grew to encompass numerous bunkers for both defence and ancilliary services, at the time of CHARIOT the next major structure of relevance would have been the Caserne des Douanes, a sizeable complex constructed within the right-angle formed by the Boulevard Paul Leferme and the Avenue du Pertuis. Standing four storeys tall the main building, in the form of a hollow trapezoid, was connected by overhead walkways to a triangular annexe on the north side of the Avenue. Although much of the Caserne was destroyed, a portion of the annexe stood until early 2005, its height and proximity to Bridge 'M' illustrating only too clearly the danger posed to Newman's northern parties by the gun platforms built onto the main structure's roof. Consisting of two single and one quadruple 20mm cannon, these enjoyed a field of fire which encompassed both the northern caisson of the 'Normandie' dock and a major portion of both main basins. With nothing of the Caserne remaining today, the scene which greets the visitor turning right into the Avenue du Pertuis is now considerably less constricting, the high walls which once thrust in from either side having been replaced by industrial development. Now a primary access road into the dockyards, the Avenue is perhaps most notable for the traffic which rumbles across Bridge 'M' (the Pont de la Douane), en-route for the northern caisson and the Avenue de la Prise d'Eau.

A substantial steel structure in its own right, which swings to one side to allow for access between the basins, Bridge 'M' can be crossed by pedestrian walkways which lead directly into the most isolated portion of the Commando operating area – a fireswept peninsula bounded by the Quai Oblique, the Quai du Pont Roulant and the Quai de la Ville Halluard. Here, in the shadow of the Caserne's guns, under fire from ships and other gun positions in the Penhoët Basin, from enemy parties hiding out on either side of the dry dock and, eventually, from the tankers penned within it, the demolition teams of Purdon, Brett and Burtinshaw laboured to prepare the northern winding house and caisson for destruction, with only Denison's tiny group for protection. Having somehow made passage from the distant Mole, it was here also that Micky Burn, waiting in vain for reinforcement, met the reconnoitring Copland prior to the general move towards Newman's HQ. The flak towers described by Micky did not survive the war; however the northern winding house destroyed by Purdon has been rebuilt, and is joined by an elongated socket to a northern caisson little changed from the days of Burtinshaw and Brett.

More properly known as a Porte Roulante, the massive dimensions of the caisson are aptly demonstrated by the busy road which runs across its upper surface. On working days one must be wary of traffic; however, this is a small price to pay for unprecedented access to a structure which is the twin of that struck by the surging *Campbeltown*. With the vast extent of the Penhoët Basin on one side and the plunging depth of the dry dock on the other, the exposure to fire of the parties working on and around the structure is immediately obvious, as indeed is the sheer scale of the task which lay before them: for at 52m in length, by 15m high and with a width of 9m, the caisson was always likely to defy all but the most extreme attempts at demolition. As a working facility the dry dock might at any time be filled, or empty – when the northern caisson offers a perfect view of its cavernous interior – or occupied by liners whose towering superstructures dwarf all but the Old Entrance bunker. Whatever the case, there is a clear line of sight towards the distant Pumping Station, along the very quayside which once rang to the sound of gunfire as Commando parties debouched from the smoking *Campbeltown*.

The quayside, which at the time of the raid contained the elongated shelters Ost 3 and Ost 4, formed the eastern extent of a triangle otherwise bounded by the Old Entrance lock and the Quai des Frégates. Containing within it the workshops of the Forges de l'Ouest, and the Ponts et Chaussées maintenance yards, Newman's men would have seen it as an untidy, menacing jumble of buildings, material stocks, fences and alleys, lit by fires and the flash of searchlights and gunfire, and containing who knows how many parties of the enemy. Altogether more open today, but with the dry dock quaysides closed, for safety reasons, to visitors, it is accessed by the long, straight run of the Avenue des Frégates, the route south followed by Copland and his party as they fought to reach Roy's bridgehead. Following in their footsteps, the constant presence of the U-Boat pens on one's right side, taken in conjunction with the confusion of structures which would then have existed on their left, imbues their succession of dashes in the open with a sense of being targets in some ghastly shooting gallery.

3: BRIDGE 'G', THE OLD ENTRANCE AND THE PUMPING STATION

The narrow neck of land forming the bridgehead, which then sat directly north of Bridge 'G', was bounded on three sides by the Quai des Frégates, the Quai de la Vieille Entrée and the northernmost socket of the Old Entrance itself. Largely devoid of cover – but clung to tenaciously nonetheless – its exposure to enemy fire from the Caserne des Douanes, the U-Boat pens, the guns on the 'Frigo' roof, and the various ships in the basin, can still be appreciated even though it has all but disappeared beneath the huge, protective Old Entrance bunker. Where once the route to and across Bridge 'G' was unobstructed, the mass of the bunker now straddles the quayside, its armoured firing ports covering the single open passage, with its own internal bridge, by means of which the Old Entrance and all points further south can now be accessed.

As with the U-Boat pens, to which it bears a striking structural similarity, the bunker now functions in support of Saint-Nazaire's developing tourism aspirations. From the Avenue de la Forme Ecluse, which runs alongside its northern face, stairs and a lift provide access to a broad slab roof with raised platforms at each extremity. The western platform, which looks out over the basins and the U-Boat complex, has positions designed to take anti-aircraft guns; while the eastern platform is surmounted by a heavily armoured turret, pierced by firing slits, from which machine-guns could dominate the Forme-Ecluse and the seaward approaches to both it and the Old Entrance. Although the bunker, begun in 1943, was never fully completed, the visitor will not be aware of any deficiencies likely to detract from its appearance ot total impregnability.

With the immediate approaches to the southern caisson [the 'Porte Roulante Aval'] and the Pumping Station closed to visitors, the eastern platform, towering as it does above the southern winding house, offers a wonderful bird's-eye view of the whole lower portion of the

From the roof of the U-Boat Pens looking east across the Saint-Nazaire Basin. The interior of the bunker on the left contains the submarine *Espadon*. The sheds on the right have replaced the Hôtel des Ponts et Chaussées.

From the site of the old ferry pier, looking west to the U-Boat Pens. The quayside where Roy maintained his bridgehead is buried beneath the massive bunker on the right.

'Normandie' dock – of caisson, socket, winding house, Pumping Station, and the stretch of shoreline beyond, below which were once underground fuel tanks, and above which sat a succession of gun positions. From this particular viewing point the successful evacuation of *Campbeltown* seems even more miraculous, given the plethora of guns able to fire directly onto her decks from almost point-blank range.

The interior of the bunker is accessed from the Avenue de la Forme Ecluse, whose broad extent contains a small parking area. In stark contrast to the grey utilitarianism of the structure's outside walls, here is a welcoming realm of comfort and modernity, containing a shop, washrooms and a reception area where those wishing to tour the interior of the submarine *Espadon* can purchase tickets. Situated within the bunker's dark and rather forbidding main chamber, this is an experience not to be missed, offering as it does a rather chastening glimpse into that tiny, equipment-packed world which, for submariners in time of war, could be both home and tomb. Her presence announced by an asdic ('sonar') 'ping' audible some distance away, *Espadon* is also a primary stop on the locally organised tours which, commencing in the U-Boat complex, take in both dockyards and the nearby Airbus facility.

On passing through the bunker to the Quai de la Vieille Entrée, the visitor will be looking across the Old Entrance to the lower of Newman's two 'islands'. With the ever-present U-Boat pens occupying much of the far side of the basin, the view ahead will be of Bridge 'G', with the lock gates and quaysides of the Old Entrance stretching away to the left. With so few boats managing to land here, this critical piece of real estate could not be destroyed as planned,

201

following the withdrawal of the northern parties. It remained under fire throughout the action, in Commando hands – but only just – with Roy and Newman maintaining a tenuous hold on both approaches.

On crossing the bridge, turn immediately left onto the southern wall of the anchorage, the Quai de Kribi, at the seaward end of which Rodier and Curtis disembarked the parties of Haines and Newman respectively. Paralleling the quayside, long and rather unprepossessing warehouses now occupy the space where once stood the considerably more elegant Hôtel des Ponts et Chaussees. Newman had fully intended to establish his HQ in the portion of this building closest to Bridge 'G', until disabused of the idea by the loss of his reserve and the unexpected presence of Germans within. With only a handful of men available he was therefore obliged to seek cover where he could command the southern bridge approaches, remaining exposed to a galling fire from the U-Boat complex until such time as Haines arrived to lob his 2″ mortar bombs onto its roof.

It is in that portion of the anchorage between the lock gates and the old ferry pier, that the various manoeuvrings took place which saw Rodier haul off to tuck ML177 under Campbeltown's quarter, Curtis bring the gunboat round to berth against the northern wall, Wynn stand by until ordered to torpedo the outer gates, and Burt and Beart stage their delayed attempts to put their Commando parties ashore.

Observing this peaceful stretch of water today, haven as it is for fishing boats and gaily coloured pleasure craft, it takes an effort of will to visualize it as it would have been when lit by searchlights, tracer and the flash of explosions – particularly so before Campbeltown's Oerlikons fell silent and her evacuated crew sought refuge on board the gunboat and MTB. Standing by the pier, the incessant clatter of gunfire to the south would have told of a continuing struggle at the Mole, but given no clue as to its likely outcome: to the left rear a rattle of small arms from the parties of Haines and Newman: on one's left hand the flash and sparkle of tracer from the dark mass of the U-Boat pens and from ships manoeuvring in the Basin: directly ahead, where the bunker now stands, more small-arms fire, the thud of grenades and the start of the sequence of explosions that would put paid to the dry dock's ancilliary equipment: the gunboat taking on board survivors while Ryder, in the shadow of the now silent Pumping Station guns, carried out his inspection of the slowly settling Campbeltown: a little to the right the battered destroyer's stern, jutting into the fairway with ML177 beside her quarter, preparing to make a run for home with Beattie and most of his officers on board: the fairway itself fast becoming a graveyard for MLs whose flaming petrol now danced eerily out in a darkness punctated by the explosion of larger calibre shells: and everywhere the multicoloured, streaking threads of tracer, much of it pouring in from the distant Pointe de Mindin, where were mounted the cannon of *Korvettenkapitän* Lothar Burhenne's *Marine-Flak-Abteilung* (MaFLA)809. In time Wynn too, having waited alongside the gunboat before discharging his torpedoes, would join Rodier in an ill-fated run for home; Burt, having at last succeeded in putting his men ashore from ML *262*, and under direct fire from the basin, would soon be obliged to take them back on board, following which his boat too would become a flaming wreck, a fate which had already overtaken Eric Beart when he attempted to nose his ML *267* onto the foreshore.

4: THE OLD MOLE AND THE PLACE DE LA VIEILLE VILLE

At the time of the fighting the rectangle of land stretching south from the Hôtel des Ponts et Chaussées to the slight elevation upon which stood the Old Town, was largely taken up with warehouses, sheds and workshops, surrounded by a network of railway lines complete with engines and scattered clusters of goods wagons. Considerably more open today, and containing within it both the Ecomusée and a large seafront car park, little now remains of the tightly-packed structures which once would have been both cover for the enemy and a barrier to Commandos seeking first to reach the Mole, and later to escape into the new town.

The north caisson, looking east. Attempts to access the interior were made via the space beneath the road surface.

Passing along the Avenue Saint-Hubert towards the Mole, the overall impression of openness and accessibility can lead to an underestimation of the task faced by Newman and his men, whose peregrinations within this general area almost always left them open to surprise attack from the flanks. Given the failures at the South Entrance and the abandonment of the northern 'island', there was nothing to prevent the Germans from feeding men across the unblown bridges, their strength and firepower therefore increasing while that of the Commandos diminished. Pinned to the shoreline north of the Mole, in the temporary cover of railway trucks, with burning MLs to their rear and the way ahead blocked by both the mass of the structures and the hostile fire which poured from within, the odds against survival, let alone escape, were so high as to make all the more remarkable the decision of Newman and Copland to engineer a breakout. Given a great deal of luck combined with the element of surprise, they might just make the Quai Demange, itself under direct fire from the 'Frigo' and the U-Boat pen roof: but then they would have to face Bridge 'D', a narrow choke-point which any competent enemy would surely deny them.

Leaving behind the car park and the shorefront Monument à L'Abolition de l'Esclavage (commemorating the abolition of slavery), the Avenue Saint-Hubert bears right to become the Avenue de la Vieille Ville at a dusty junction much favoured by players of 'Boules'. During the raid this highly exposed position, a crossroads in more senses than one, remained 'hot' throughout the fighting, swept by fire from the Old Town, the Mole and the far side of Bridge 'D'. For the visitor facing south, the area of foreshore occupied immediately prior to the breakout will be to the left rear: to the left front, the Old Mole conceals its brush with death and danger behind a facade of timeless tranquility: directly ahead is the rise of the Old Town: and to the right the Place de la Vieille Ville stretches away towards the commercial centre of Saint-Nazaire. Having already proved impassable to the parties of Walton and Watson this, the quickest and most obvious path towards freedom, was wisely discounted in favour of the long right hook towards Bridge 'G' and the Quai Demange.

Jutting some 115m out into the river, its upper surface defined by low walls which run along each edge, the Mole's obvious attractions as a landing point belie the series of deficiencies which combined on the night to destroy all chances of putting the GROUP 1 parties ashore. Surmounted by a lighthouse which remains today, and two substantial pill-boxes, long since demolished, it was to all intents and purposes barred to anyone attempting to land at other than the

Looking north along the west quay of the South Entrance to what was Bridge D. The Old Entrance bunker is in view to the right rear. The Rue du Port runs along the left side.

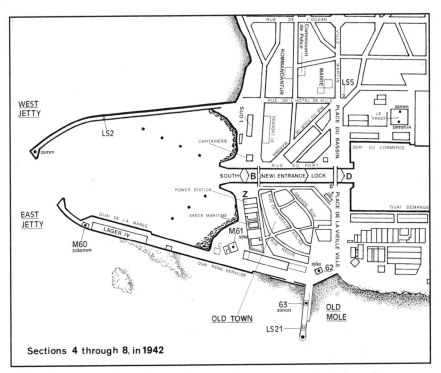

Sections 4 through 8, in 1942

slipway running along its northern face. Immediately below the lighthouse and to either side of it, steps do run down to the water: indeed some of ML*192's* survivors used those on the south side (whose stone face is pockmarked still) to access the upper surface and, having done so, Micky Burn then somehow or other managed to make his way shorewards. But as a site for assault in numbers their steep and narrow dimensions would, by precluding the passage of troops in other than single-file, have created a situation in which men could be picked off one by one as they emerged from the darkness below. Walking the slipway at full tide today, its broad expanse and gentle slope might appear to have made it eminently suitable for MLs seeking to come alongside: but the truth is that as the tide begins to fall the speedy appearance of rocks and muddy sand indicates just how shallow is the actual depth beneath the surface. Of the three MLs actually to approach the structure, only *457* got in as planned, the attempts of *447* and *307* both being inhibited by grounding.

At a time and in a place where speed was of the essence, unexpected navigational difficulties only exacerbated an already dire situation for MLs, probably already damaged, which were illuminated by the searchlight on the foremost of the two pill-boxes, and under fire from the cannon atop its twin directly above the slipway, from a gun at the base of the Mole, from troops sheltering behind the low walls, from the guns on the eastern arm of the Avant Port, and from the batteries across on the far estuary shore. With access already so restricted, it only took a couple of blazing boats to block the route in and bring home to other COs the fact that, by hanging around, they too were risking destruction to no purpose. Sadly, given the strength of the structure's defences, the obvious importance attached to its capture was not reflected in the resources committed, only the gunboat possessing the firepower necessary to achieve a temporary local ascendancy.

5: THE AVANT PORT, 'SANTÉ MARITIME' AND POWER STATION COMPLEX

On leaving the Mole, **turn immediately left** onto the Quai René Kerviler. Here, in the right-angle between the two structures is the stretch of water which saw the demise of Stephens' ML *192*, the crippled boat having slewed behind *Campbeltown* and across the bow of ML *447* to strike the south face of the Mole and drift away with the tide, blazing furiously. While some of those fortunate enough to escape the consuming flames did strike out for the lighthouse steps, the main group of survivors, led by Stephens himself, reached and climbed onto this quayside where they were captured shortly thereafter.

Following the quayside southwards brings the visitor to the junction of the short Avenue du Quai des Marées and the innermost portion of the Avant Port, whose east and west arms curve away towards the lighthouses whose misidentification on the night almost brought

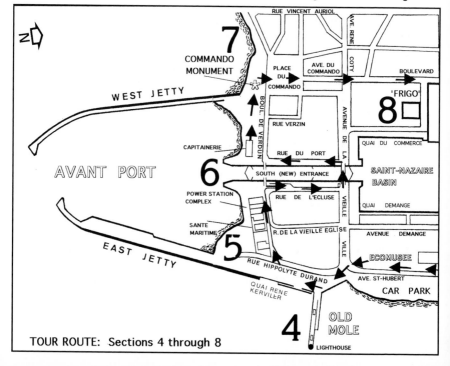

TOUR ROUTE: Sections 4 through 8

Campbeltown's odyssey to a swift and tragic conclusion. The East Jetty is the broader of the two, its inner face identified as the Quai des Marées. At its widest portion, out towards the lighthouse (Feu Est), once stood the warehouse Lager 1V, directly next to which was the commanding gun position M60. On the far side of the anchorage, stretching back from the Feu Ouest, the rather narrower West Jetty was surmounted by both a 20mm cannon and the searchlight position LS2.

The Avenue du Quai des Marées leads towards the rise of the Old Town passing, on the left, the large bunker which once held cannon M61. Now incorporated into adjoining development, this ugly, utilitarian mass of concrete speaks only of menace, standing as it does so close to the altogether more humanitarian 'Santé

Looking along the Old Mole, showing the slipway on the left, and the low walls used for shelter by the defending troops. The far shore was the position of the 809th Flak Battalion *MaFLA809*.

Maritime' – which building was struck by 'overs' directed towards the gun.

At the junction with the Rue Hippolyte Durand, with the heights of the Old Town immediately in front, **turn left** towards swing bridge 'B', a primary target on the night which, as it was not destroyed, later became a main access route for German reinforcements pouring across the South Entrance. Here, along the left side of the street, remain two important structures, both of which survived the post-raid laying waste of Old Saint-Nazaire. The first of these – more advantageously viewed from the Rue de la Vieille Eglise, on the high ground immediately above – is the 'Santé Maritime' or, more properly, the Service de Sanitaire Maritime, which legend is still in evidence today. It was in the basement, denoted 'Poste de Secours Santé Maritime', that Dr. Edmond Bizard prepared for the worst in the aid post staffed by himself, Sector Chief Joseph Richaume, two nurses and four stretcher-bearers, one of whom was his son Alain.

Between the 'Santé' and the bridge, occupying most of the corner where the South Entrance opens out into the Avant Port, is the substantial red-brick complex housing – as its over-door legends still proclaim – the Usine Elévatoire and the Usine Electrique. Yet another of the many targets assigned to GROUP 1, its destruction was the responsibility of demolition party 1D, working within an area hopefully 'cleared' by Bertie Hodgson, while Ronnie Swayne's team took care of the bridge and lock-gates nearby.Having escaped the depradations of both the war and the hasty reconstruction which followed, the complex seems ignorant of the passage of time, its tall smokestack stretching skyward, its south face shielding from view yet another ugly post-raid concrete bunker.

6: THE SOUTH ENTRANCE (BRIDGES 'B' AND 'D') AND OLD TOWN SITE

From the quayside next to the eastern end of Bridge 'B' – now a single-lane, light-controlled thoroughfare – with the site of the Old Town rising to one's right, there is an excellent view along the whole length of this most southerly lock towards lifting-bridge 'D'. The value of seizing and destroying the crossings is immediately obvious in that this natural 'moat' would have secured the whole southern island as a base from which to stage a successful re-embarkation. Also immediately obvious, however, are both the inhibiting scale of the structures to be destroyed by such small parties, and the vulnerability of Commandos exposed on this eastern quayside to fire from streets on the far side which in those days were angled away from the lock, providing excellent cover for the approach of enemy parties.

From this point continue northwards, climbing gently up to a junction on the elevated area which once held the maze of narrow streets and alleys comprising the Old Town. Here the visitor can choose to go left, following the Rue de l'Ecluse along the lockside to the strongly girdered mass of bridge 'D'; or swing immediately right and take advantage of the curving Rue de la Vieille Eglise – substantially realigned since the time of Pritchard's death – with its commanding view southwards over the 'Santé'. Both routes will lead to the lateral Avenue de la Vieille Ville, the primary access route from the main town into this southern portion of the dockyard, and the road which biscects that deadly rectangle known to Newman and his men as the Place de la Vieille Ville (Old Town Square).

Bordered to east and west by water, its northern extent deliniated

The Santé Maritime, 2005. One of the few buildings in this area to survive the war. The basement was in use as an aid-post at the time of the raid.

by the warehouse area and its southern edge butting against the Old Town, the impenetrability of this broad, open space was a key feature of CHARIOT, the automatic fire which swept across it deterring all attempts to force a passage. Containing, as it does, the approaches to the all-important lifting bridge, it was its western portion which saw most of the action on the night – particularly from the point at which the southern face, rather than remaining square to the bridge as it does today, cut back sharply towards the lock-gates shown as target 'C' (now removed).

In the corner space left by the angled frontage the Germans built shelter Ost 6, whose northernmost projection was close to the Café Moderne, the French establishment pressed into service as a 'holding tank' for wounded such as Watson, Bradley and Chant. To the left, or west, of Ost 6, stood the small concrete structure behind which Pritchard and his team sheltered prior to sinking the two tugs moored at the Quai de la Vieille Ville, and prior to his ill-fated patrol of the Old Town. And directly opposite the shelter site still stretches the dreadfully exposed Quai Demange, against which the flotilla of minesweepers had originally been moored and along which Newman's column somehow forced a passage in the face of everything the enemy could throw at them.

Moving onto Bridge 'D', a counterbalanced lifting bridge, or Pont Basculant, pivoted on the far quayside, two things are immediately obvious: first, the unfeasibility of ever destroying so large a target with man-packed explosives alone; and second, how perfect a 'killing ground' it should have made for troops defending so narrow a frontage against lightly-armed Commandos, short of ammunition and nursing a high proportion of wounded. Given well-trained men and competent leadership, Newman's surge, however spirited, should have been halted then and there: but it was not, and in the face of a poorly organized defence, through grenade blasts and sparking ricochets, he and his remaining men won through to the main town and to the possibility – however transitory – of freedom.

Having gained the far side of the bridge the Commandos found themselves in the capacious Place du Bassin, a long, rectangular square very much the twin of that from which they had just escaped. Unfortunately their own arrival coincided with that of stronger and better-trained enemy reinforcements, leaving them with no alternative but to break left into the labyrinth of streets which then ran westward between the now impassable square and the seafront.

Turning into the Rue du Port today, the visitor is faced with regularly proportioned and rather bland new build, courtesy of the devastation caused by bombing. Gone are sharply angled streets such as the Rue des Sables and the Rue du Four de Marsain, which in those days would have punctuated the right-hand frontage: gone is the elegant two-storey wartime *Capitainerie*, or harbour-master's Office, which stood at the corner of the Rue du Port and what was then the Boulevard du Maréchal Pétain: and gone also is the elevation, so familiar to returning submariners, upon which crowds of soldiers, sailors, female auxiliaries and the like would gather to welcome home salt-stained boats flying their victory pennants. Largely silent now, it is perhaps hard to imagine how, when U-Boats were in the ascendant and before Lancasters and Fortresses reduced the surrounding buildings to broken teeth of rubble, the quayside on the left once rang to the sound of bands, the thrum of diesels and the shouted commands of crisply turned-out honour guards.

7: THE MONUMENT DU COMMANDO/ PLACE DU COMMANDO

At the lower end of the Rue du Port, turn right into what is now the Boulevard de Verdun. From this point, with the base of the west jetty of the Avant Port – where survivors of the fight between ML *306* and *Jaguar* were gathered before being transported out of town – on one's left hand, it is only a short walk past the site of the large shelter 'Sud 1', to the tall, granite column which marks the site of the Monument du Commando. Unveiled on 2 August, 1947 by M. Ramadier, the Premier of France, the column surmounts a panel upon which are inscribed the names of all those raiders who lost their lives. During a ceremony attended by veterans and numerous dignitaries, the Mayor of Saint-Nazaire gave a speech in which he commented meaningfully of the fallen that: 'Your sons have become also the sons of France'. Completing the CHARIOT memorial is *Campbeltown's* forward gun, dredged from the harbour some thirty years after being blown from her foredeck. Mounted on a plinth to one side of the granite column, the curvature of its heavy barrel gives some clue as to the force of the explosion which ripped the old destroyer apart.

Erected on the foreshore close to a broad, sandy beach, the Commando column is only one of several memorials which, dating from both World Wars, stretch westwards along the Boulevard. Standing close by the granite column, another inscribed panel recalls the tragedy of the *Lancastria*, sunk on 17 June 1940, with such heavy loss of life that news with the potential to damage morale on the Home Front was suppressed until such time as the *New York Times* broke the story on 26 July: a little further along can be found the French tribute to their own war dead, the Monument aux Morts: while, appearing to rise out of the sea opposite the distant Jardin des Plantes is the tall and very striking Mémorial Américain – a rock pillar topped by a statue in bronze of an eagle, wings outstretched, which carries on its back a 'doughboy' with sword in hand. Dating from 1926, the original was blown up by the Germans following America's entry into the war on the grounds that it was too provocative.

From the Commando memorial cross the Boulevard to the Rue de l'Ancien Hôtel de Ville, whose name speaks of the substantial changes which have overtaken this part of town. The Rue follows the right-hand side of what is now an open space called the Place du Commando. Completely built-up at the time of the raid, this was hardly the best choice of 'escape route' for Newman's tired and isolated parties, containing as it did both the *Kommandantur* and the *Commissariat de Police*. At the north-east corner of the square, where the Rue carries on to join with the Avenue René Coty, the visitor passes the original location of the Hôtel de Ville whose cellars, during the raid, contained the Command Post of the Défense Passive, under that civilian organization's Director, M. Roger Campredon.

8: THE 'FRIGO': RETURN TO THE U-BOAT PENS

The junction with the Avenue René Coty marks the westernmost extension of the wartime Place du Bassin, close to searchlight position LS5. It was the appearance, at this particular point, of German reinforcements, which had caused the Commandos to break left after successfully carrying Bridge 'D'.Crossing the busy road returns the visitor to the Boulevard de la Légion d'Honneur, and the U-Boat complex, close to the southern face of which is the modern home of the Entrepôt Frigorifique ('Frigo'), whose wartime, flat-roofed incarnation carried two cannon positions, a single 20mm mounting to the west, and a quadruple 20mm directly overlooking Bridge 'D' and the Quai Demange. Taken in conjunction with the commanding position offered by the nearby concrete roof above the completed pens, these could hardly have been more ideally placed to disrupt Commando activities, the weight of fire they could direct towards the route of withdrawal only adding to the mystique surrounding Newman's successful breakout.

Having now completed the tour, perhaps the main impression garnered by a circuit of the locks, docks and quaysides which such tiny parties had been expected to first assault and then control in the face of a far more numerous enemy, will be one of amazement that they were able to survive at all when so exposed to heavy fire they could do little to suppress. Especially bearing in mind how only the GROUP 3 parties managed to land in any strength, the Commandos' successful neutralization of the 'Normandie' dock must surely stand as a glowing tribute both to their spirit and training, and to the doggedness of those at home who continued to fight for the very existence of such contentious elites.

APPENDIX 2

SAINT-NAZAIRE: ADVICE FOR VISITORS

Saint-Nazaire is today a town of almost 70,000 inhabitants; a 'sous-préfecture' of the Department 'Loire-Atlantique', itself an administrative area within the region known as the 'Pays de la Loire'. It is situated immediately below the southernmost boundary of Brittany, a region with which it shares much in the way of culture and history, and through which it will be approached by most British visitors accessing the area by road.

Stretching along the northern shore of the broad, shallow estuary, where the 1000km long River Loire – having passed through Nevers, Orléans, Tours, Angers and Nantes – flows into the Bay of Biscay, its industrial heart is very much at odds both with the vineyards, chalk gorges and imposing chateaux of the Loire itself, and with estuary shores where elegant resorts and villas dress stretches of low cliffs punctuated by some of the finest beaches in France.

Just a few kilometres west of Saint-Nazaire is Saint-Marc-sur-Mer, where the director Jacques Tati shot the quintessentially French movie 'Les Vacances de Monsieur Hulot': and, continuing along the coast road one comes to the fashionable and ever-expanding La Baule, with its seven kilometres of golden sand backed by a broad and imposing promenade. Now a favourite weekend retreat of Parisians who can reach its imposing station from Paris, Gare Montparnasse, in only three and a half hours by TGV [Train à Grande Vitesse – www.tgv.co.uk], it was home during wartime to various German headquarters and to U-Boat crews being rested, in accordance with orders, well out of harm's way. In his book *Hitler's U-Boat Bases*, the author Jak P Mallmann Showell describes how hotels and other establishments were taken over by the U-flotillas, with the Casino in use as a theatre and mess, the Hôtel Royal home to the 7th Flotilla's communications centre, the Hôtel Celtic providing accommodation and mess facilities for the flotilla's officers, and the Hôtel Majestik as Flotilla HQ. Of primary concern to the sailors and Commandos wounded during CHARIOT, would be the elegant and substantial Hôtel Hermitage, converted early on into a naval sanatorium. Described today as 'a grand white Anglo-Norman manor with a half-timbered facade' (www.cybevasion.fr), the four-star Hermitage remains a dominant feature of the western seafront.

As with so much of the Biscay coast, the villas, beaches, cliffs and sands share pride of place with concrete and steel reminders of the importance once attached to town and estuary by a Reich under seige. These fortifications were begun immediately after the fall of France, and were developed and strengthened throughout the war years as Saint-Nazaire and its surrounding area was promoted from U-Boat base to the mightily defended fortress 'pocket' which, though invested by American troops in the wake of the breakout from Normandy, was never overrun. Ranging in size from machine-gun posts and the circular concrete gunpits known as 'Tobruks', all the way to the massive casements of the Fort de l'Eve, Le Pointeau and La Pointe de Saint-Gildas, these dot the coastline still; sullen, grey 'Marie Celestes' which, having once buzzed with life, are now brought down by time and rust, the salt wind having all but erased their once prominent Deutsche Schrift insignia.

Within Saint-Nazaire itself the greatest evidence of war is the modernity of the structures one sees around, a new town having grown from the sea of rubble which greeted returning Nazairiens in 1945-6, and from which – or so it seemed – protruded only fortifications. Having been expanded and augmented following Operation CHARIOT, in line with the new priority given to the construction of the *Atlantikwall*, these littered the dockyard area, their sheer scale causing many to be just as impervious to French attempts at post-war demolition as they had been to Allied bombs. As a consequence of their resilience, the area of the town's docks and basins is, today, the one portion of the habitation to retain much of its wartime integrity and atmosphere: and it is on this area – the field of battle for Charles Newman's Army Commandos – that this guide concentrates, its twin ambitions being, to convey to the reader a very real sense of what the men of CHARIOT were up against, and to promote a better appreciation of the skill, courage and self-sacrifice which saw them through to success.

As detailed in Appendix 1, the battlefield is best toured in the form of a circle beginning and ending within the U-Boat complex, which vast structure houses the Tourist Office, and outside which there is plenty of parking. The tour is best done on foot: however those wishing to drive will find that access is open and easy, and that its course contains several parking areas. There are washrooms in both the pen complex and the bunker which houses the submarine *Espadon*: and because the main basins are close to the centre of town – being only a short walk from several hotels – there are a plethora of shops and restaurants nearby. The elevated viewing platforms atop the U-Boat pens and Old Entrance bunker offer magnificent views: however, in hot weather these should be visited early in the day as the temperature later on can easily exceed thirty degrees Celsius – this a consequence of the concrete reflecting accumulated heat: As the dock area can also become uncomfortably hot on breathless days, it is advisable to carry mineral water – and plenty of it.

The walking tour itself takes from two to three hours: however this time can be expanded greatly if advantage is taken of the various exhibitions and tours available to visitors within the same geographical area. Detailed information on all of these can be obtained on site, or in advance, from the Tourist Information Office within the pen complex on the Boulevard de la Légion d'Honneur, Base sous-marine, BP173, 44613 Saint-Nazaire Cedex. Telephone – 02 40 22 40 65: fax – 02 40 22 19 80. E-mails should be directed to – contact@saint-nazaire-tourisme.com. An English language web-page can be found at www.saint-nazaire-tourisme.com [All telephone/fax numbers contained in the guide are presented in their standard French ten-digit format: to use these numbers from within the UK, discard the first 0, and prefix the remaining nine-digit number with the area code 00 33]

In recognition of the port's shipbuilding heritage, the primary exhibition is *Escal'Atlantic* – a tribute to the many great ocean liners which were constructed in the yards across from the Saint-Nazaire Basin. This has been constructed within the U-Boat pens, and involves a tour through various 'decks' which concludes with visitors being 'evacuated' into the water below by means of a lifeboat slung from davits.

The Tourism office can also arrange for visitors to tour the various dockyard manufacturing facilities, in a voyage of exploration which includes Alstom-Chantiers de l'Atlantique, the builders of *Queen Mary 2*, and the Airbus factory.

One of the most arresting exhibits is the 1,600-ton decommissioned French submarine *Espadon* (Swordfish), a boat which dates from 1957. One of the original 'Narval' class of submarines, *Espadon* was the first French boat to cross beneath the polar icefields. She was donated to Saint-Nazaire in 1986 and rests, today, within the dark interior of the Old Entrance bunker. Tours of the boat are self-guided, the claustrophobic interior giving the impression of having been packed with every item of equipment that could possibly be fitted in, and promoting deep respect for those who could live and work within such a confined space.

Within the area defined by the walking tour, the last exhibits are to be found within the Ecomusée, a modern structure situated just south of Colonel Newman's HQ position in an area which, during 1942, was packed tight with stores, warehouses and workshops. The Ecomusée is, in essence, a local museum which offers a voyage through an illustrated history of Saint-Nazaire. The museum has a number of fine collections which can be accessed by researchers who book in advance, these including excellent photographs of Saint-Nazaire before, during and after the Second World War. For contact details, see under Museums.

Travelling to Saint-Nazaire/Advice on driving:
Visitors wishing to access Saint-Nazaire by air, can take advantage of flights between several UK/Irish destinations and Nantes, currently being offered by British Airways (www.britishairways.com), Air France (www.airfrance.com), and Ryanair (www.ryanair.com). The small, modern airport just south of Nantes, (www.nantes.aeroport.fr), offers car hire on site, taxis and a regular 'Tan Air' shuttle into the heart of the city, stopping opposite the main railway station from which it is only a short journey into Saint-Nazaire itself. Tickets can be purchased at the station (a return ticket is an 'aller retour') or arranged in advance from www.raileurope.co.uk As always, travellers are reminded to validate their tickets before boarding any French train, by stamping them in the orange machines which are to be found by platform entrances.

Although Saint-Nazaire is some way from the Channel ferry ports, its proximity to Brittany makes accessing it by car anything but a chore. An excellent system of routes nationale allow for both rapid progress where time is of the essence, or for easy access to the region's coastline, historic ports and contemplative countryside. The closest ferry ports are St Malo, at 196km from Saint-Nazaire, and Roscoff, at 276km. Caen is 322 km from the port, Cherbourg 358km, Le Havre 402km, and Calais a distant 663km. In the case of Calais, the short ferry crossing has to be weighed against an almost inevitable overnight stay en-route: however, it, Caen, Cherbourg and le Havre all bring visitors within range of the Normandy beaches. The principal ferry operators are – Brittany Ferries (www.brittanyferries.com), UK telephone 08703 665 333; and P & O (www.poferries.com) , UK main switchboard 08705 980 333.

A number of internet sites, such as www.mappy.com offer free, comprehensive route plans; while www.driving.drive-alive.co.uk also offers a wealth of useful information on such topics as driving rules and regulations, and French road signs. Bearing in mind the potential for confusion inherent in trying to communicate detail in an unfamiliar language, one should always have a camera to hand in the case of accidents (perhaps a disposable camera tucked away in the glovebox), and relevant papers organized for easy display. When stopped late one evening at a police check, I found that having passport, licence, insurance and registration documents filed within plastic sleeves in a ring-binder made for a speedy and fuss-free departure. As traffic offences – such as speeding or having lights non operative – can result in either on-the-spot fines or even confiscation of your licence, it is strongly advised that the following basic rules are followed. As blood-alcohol limits in France are lower than in Britain, do not drink and drive: carry a spare-bulb kit, a warning triangle and a first-aid kit: keep to speed limits, as radar traps are not infrequent occurences: if your car does not have Euro plates, make sure a GB sticker is displayed on the rear: and always make sure your headlights have been converted with adhesive lens adaptors. A Green Card is no longer necessary; but you must carry a driving licence valid within the EU, a certificate of motor insurance to prove you are covered within the EU (comprehensive policies are advised), and a V5C document to prove you are the registered keeper of the vehicle. In terms of personal health, new European Health Insurance Cards cards are being issued to replace the E111 document which gave basic coverage within many European countries. Remember that this is basic coverage, and bearing in mind the costs involved in repatriating you, your passengers, or your vehicle to the UK, this should be supplemented with additional travel insurance. While it is always sensible to make sure your vehicle is fully roadworthy before travelling abroad, European breakdown cover can be a very worthwhile investment.

www.franceguide.com is an excellent source of information on almost every aspect of travel within France – including special needs travel and links to rail services such as the TGV (click on 'Practical Information'). www.brittanytourism.com is an English language source of tourist information for the region in general, www.westernloire.com performing the same function for the area immediately surrounding Saint-Nazaire. For those who would prefer to let someone else do the driving, the War Research Society [www.battlefieldtours.co.uk] organize an annual tour which takes in both Saint-Nazaire and the Normandy beaches. Their knowledgeable guide is also a member of the Saint-Nazaire Society [www.stnazairesociety.org]

Maps: Atlases: Street Plans.
In this part of France there is simply so much to see that having the right maps available is a must. For those travelling by car, the ferry company websites provide helpful terminal plans, and the various Tourism offices are an abundant source of generalized tourist maps. Beyond these, however, there is no sustitute for a large-scale road atlas either of France in general, or of the area through which you will be passing. Ideally you should be looking for a scale of around 4 miles to the inch (1:250,000) as, particularly with motorways, this is large enough to show service and rest areas, and tolls. Bearing in mind the difficulties inherent in unfolding or opening large maps, an A4 version is preferable, one such being the *AA Road Atlas* to France, which uses information drawn from IGN, the French national mapping agency. The 'maps and guides' section within the 'franceguide' website at – www.franceguide.com – is an excellent source of useful information.

For the area around Saint-Nazaire, covering both shores of the estuary, the IGN 'Top 25' series of tourist maps is ideal. At a scale of 1:25,000, these are sufficiently detailed to show forts, casemates and pill-boxes. 1022ET – ST-NAZAIRE, covers the port itself, the northern road and rail approaches and the Parc Naturel Régional de Brière: 1023OT – LA BAULE, covers the north shore of the estuary from Saint-Marc-sur-Mer through La Baule-Escoublac and Batz-sur-Mer, to Le Croisic: and 1123OT – ST-NAZAIRE PORNIC, covers the southern shore from St-Brévin-les-Pins through Pointe de St-Gildas to Pornic. For getting around within port and town, IGN also produce an indexed street plan of Saint-Nazaire, at a scale of 1:12,500: its reference number is 72235. IGN maps can be obtained direct from the Institut Géographique National, at www.ign.fr (catalogue available), or from UK sources such as the Hereford Map centre Ltd, telephone 01432 266322: e-mail sales@themapcentre.com www.themapcentre.com For those who prefer an interactive experience, a moveable, zoomable street plan, with video images, can be found at www.plan-saintnazaire.fr

Bearing in mind the lengthy German occupation of this area, numerous books have been published locally which deal with particular aspects and experiences of the war years. While almost exclusively written in French, many are illustrated to the degree where their maps and photographs can still be very useful indeed to the persistent researcher. While it can be difficult – if not impossible – to source these easily from the UK, they can be purchased in and around Saint-Nazaire, particularly so from the two specifically military museums mentioned below.

Museums

Mention has already been made of the Ecomusée within Saint-Nazaire itself. While this presents an excellent record of the origins and development of the port and town, it lacks the particular military focus of the two sites detailed below. The museum is situated on the Avenue de Saint-Hubert, 44600 Saint-Nazaire, close to a car park. Telephone number – 02 51 10 03 03: fax – 02 51 10 12 03: e-mail – ecomusee@mairie-saintnazaire.fr: web – www.ecomusee-saint-nazaire.com

On the northern shore of the Loire estuary, between la Baule and Croisic, stands the substantial German command bunker which is home to Le Grand Blockhaus War Museum (Musée de la Poche de Saint-Nazaire). Once disguised as a house, complete with painted windows and false roof, its several compartments are now dedicated to preserving the memory of Saint-Nazaire during the war years. The museum can be contacted by mail, at Le Grand Blockhaus, Côte Sauvage, 44740 Batz-sur-Mer. Telephone/fax number – 02 40 23 88 29: e-mail – grand-blockhaus@wanadoo.fr. While there is a French language web site at http://perso.wanadoo.fr/grand.blockhaus access details in English can be obtained via www.brittanytourism.com by typing Grand Blockhaus into the search box.

Although it does not relate specifically to Saint-Nazaire, visitors with their own transport will be rewarded by visiting St Marcel, just off the N 166, between Ploërmel and the picture-book village of Rochefort-en-Terre. Here is to be found the Musée de la Résistance Bretonne, an airy modern construction whose halls contain a wonderful collection of wartime artifacts and memorabilia. Officially dedicated to the memory of local resistants – the 'maquis' of Saint-Marcel – who engaged in battle with German forces during June, 1944, the museum is in fact a record of the wartime experience of Brittany as a whole, including U-Boat bases such as Saint-Nazaire. Static displays are supplemented by audio-visual presentations and a well-stocked bookshop. The grounds contain a cafe and a wide range of military vehicles – some of which are equipped to carry visitors during the holiday season. The (French language) web site at www.resistance-bretonne.com contains an e-mail contact form. Telephone number – 02 97 75 16 90: fax – 02 97 75 16 92.

Hotels in and around Saint-Nazaire

With the area around Saint-Nazaire, particularly westwards from Saint-Marc-sur-Mer to La Baule, being a very popular holiday destination, there is no shortage of places to stay. The coastal resorts are, undoubtedly, beautiful: however, for visitors wishing to concentrate on Saint-Nazaire's wartime history, commuting to and from the port along narrow and often busy roads can soon become a chore. Far better to concentrate on hotels, apartments and camping sites within, or on the outskirts of, the town, a selection of which are given below. For a full listing go to the following English language websites, at:

www.mairie-saintnazaire.fr/decouvrir/english/infoprat_eng.htm
www.cybevasion.com/hotels/france/hotels_saint-nazaire_18163.html

Hôtel Restaurant Aquilon*** 2 Rue Michel-Ange, Rond-Point Océanis 44600 Saint-Nazaire: south-western outskirts, within easy reach of the Fort de l'Eve, and the north shore. Telephone – 02 51 76 67 66: e-mail – contact@hotel-aquilon.com: web – www.hotelaquilon.com

Hôtel Restaurant le Berry*** 1 Place Pierre Semard, (Face a la Gare), 44600 Saint-Nazaire: as its name suggests, situated close by the railway station at the northern end of the Avenue de la République. Telephone – 02 40 22 42 61: e-mail – berry.hotel@wanadoo.fr: web – www.hotel-du-berry.fr

Hôtel au Bon Accueil*** 39 Rue Francois Marceau, 44600 Saint-Nazaire: situated by a small square within easy walking distance of the U-Boat complex. Telephone – 02 40 22 07 05: e-mail – au-bon-accueil44@wanadoo.fr

Hôtel Restaurant de la Plage*** Plage de Monsieur Hulot, 37 Rue du Commandant Charcot, 44600 Saint-Marc-sur-Mer: south-western outskirts, on the north shore, close by the Fort de l'Eve, beaches and coastal path. Telephone – 02 40 91 99 01: e-mail – hotel.de.la.plage@wanadoo.fr: web – www.hotel-de-la-plage-44.com

Quality Suites Saint-Nazaire*** 47 Boulevard de la Libération, 44600 Saint-Nazaire: apartments situated towards the north side of town, close to the port and about ten-fifteen minutes walk from the U-Boat complex. Telephone – 02 40 00 64 88: fax – 02 28 54 14 15: e-mail – contact@resideatlantique.com: web www.saintnazaire.quality-hotel.fr

Camping de l'Eve** Route du Fort de l'Eve: immediately opposite the bunkers of the Fort de l'Eve and the Plage de la Courance. Telephone – 02 40 91 90 65: fax – 02 40 91 76 59

ESCOUBLAC-LA-BAULE WAR CEMETERY

The lovingly-tended 'Cimetière Anglais' is to be found a little inland from the seafront at La Baule, set amidst the modern villas which line the Route de la Ville Halgand. Maintained by the Commonwealth War Graves Commission, the site dates from the early years of World War Two and is the last resting place of fifty-six named 'Charioteers'. Containing a total of 329 burials – 74 of which remain unidentified – the cemetery also contains the graves of airmen shot down during the many raids on the area, and servicemen lost both prior to the retreats of 1940 and when the troopship *Lancastria* was sunk offshore on 17 June, 1940.

ACKNOWLEDGEMENTS

Central to the writing of any book which purports to tell the story of Operation CHARIOT, is the support, encouragement and accumulated wisdom of the members and associate members of the St Nazaire Society. Consisting not only of those soldiers and sailors who participated in the raid, but also of families and friends, the Society is a primary source of experience gained at first hand, the fruits of which have been made available to me in the course of numerous interviews, and through personal narratives from which I have been permitted to quote freely. The comprehensive Society newsletters, produced in recent years by Eric de la Torre, MBE., have proven to be a rich vein of information, the collection steadily coalescing into a unique historical record.

In the case of individual narratives, I owe a special debt of thanks to Dr W H Watson, MBE., MC, for allowing me to access his unpublished personal memoir; to Peter Copland for making available his father's excellent account of the raid, the letter he wrote to his wife Ethel immediately prior to the raid, and his invaluable photographic record of 2 Commando in Scotland, during 1941; to the Reverend Canon Lisle Ryder for permission to quote from Captain Robert Ryder VC's extensive written records of CHARIOT, and to publish photographs of HMS *Campbeltown* during conversion; and to the family of Lieutenant Colonel Charles Newman VC for supplying me with a copy of his detailed action report, written while still a POW. In the case of Lieutenant Stuart Chant – later Lieutenant Colonel Stuart Chant-Sempill, OBE., MC – although his personal recollections took the form of a book his son, Lieutenant Colonel Ian Chant-Sempill, has volunteered a significant and very pertinent volume of background documentation, this including the short, quoted account which I have attributed to F A Carr, DCM (Sergeant, 5 Cdo).

Other written accounts which contribute directly to this text have been sourced from – F W M Arkle (Sub Lieutenant, RNVR, ML *177*), D K Croft (Able Seaman, RANR, ML *307*), Colonel W W Etches, OBE., MC (Lieutenant, 3 Cdo), F A Smith, DSM (Able Seaman, RN, MGB *314*), E C A Roberts, OBE, FIB (Sub Lieutenant, RNVR, ML *262*), G R Wheeler, MM (Corporal, 2 Cdo), the family of I L Maclagan (Corporal, 9 Cdo), and E D Stogdon (Sub Lieutenant, RNVR, HMS *Tynedale*) – whose insight into both the attack on *U-593* and the subsequent confrontation with the German Torpedo-Boat flotilla has proved invaluable.

I have Mrs Elmslie Henderson to thank for references to her late husband, Nigel Tibbits, DSC (Lieutenant, RN HMS *Campbeltown*) contained in Lieutenant Commander Beattie's letter to her, of 28 June, 1945. And I am indebted to *Radio Times* for allowing me to quote extracts from the article 'My Town is St Nazaire', 29 April, 1949. The short quotation from Professor F H Hinsley's second volume of 'British Intelligence in the Second World War' is Crown Copyright material reproduced with the permission of the Controller of HMSO and the Queen's printer for Scotland. And Jerome M O'Connor's description of the general layout of U-Boat pens is quoted with the permission of the US Naval Institute.

As ever, the various departments of the Imperial War Museum, in London, have proven to be a primary source of Crown Copyright material which includes both photographs and highly relevant documentation. I would like to express my gratitude to the Trustees for having been permitted to access, and quote from, a selection of after-action reports including Lieutenant Commander Beattie's 'Narrative of HMS *Campbeltown* at St Nazaire', and Lieutenant Commander Tweedie's 'Action Report of HMS *Tynedale*, 31 March, 1942'.

Other reports directly related to this text include those written by – Lieutenant Dunstan Curtis, RNVR, DSC., CdeG.,CO of MGB *314*; Lieutenant Ted Burt, RNVR, DSC., CO of ML *262*; Sub Lieutenant N G Machin, RNVR, DSC., First Lieutenant, ML *156*; Lieutenant T D L Platt, RNR, DSO., normally CO of ML *443*, but acting as CO of ML *447* during the raid; Lieutenant K M Horlock, RNVR, temporarily acting as CO of ML *443*; Sub Lieutenant N R Nock, RNVR, DSC., CO of ML *298*; and Sub Lieutenant R C M V Wynn, RNVR, DSC., CO of MTB *74*.

In respect of information communicated orally, I have relied, to varying degrees, on taped interviews with – Herr Gerd Kelbling (*Kapitänleutnant, U-593*); Lieutenant Colonel Bob Montgomery, MC., (Captain, RE, Special Service Brigade); Bob Wright (Sapper Corporal, 12Cdo); Arthur Ashcroft (Private, 2 Cdo); Don Randall, DCM., (Lance Sergeant, 2 Cdo); and Des Chappell (Lance Sergeant, 1 Cdo). Needless to say, all material gleaned from interviews has contributed to the whole, even if not mentioned specifically here.

Over the years a number of 'Charioteers' have published personal histories such as allow for a more comprehensive depiction of their part in, and impressions of, the raid. Special mention is due to those publishers and, or, authors who have allowed passages to be quoted freely in the text. Generous, as always, Major General Corran Purdon, CBE., MC., CPM., has placed no restriction on my use of his 1993 publication, *List the Bugle*: while Michael Burn, MC., and his publisher, Michael Russell have afforded me the same courtesy with respect to Micky's 2003, *Turned Towards the Sun*.

In providing photographs, and detailed information and drawings relevant to my understanding of the construction and performance of the vessels which carried the attacking force to Saint-Nazaire, special thanks are due to Al Ross and John Lambert: the former particularly for allowing me to adapt his profiles of HMS *Campbeltown*, and the latter for his exquisitely detailed small boat plans and weapon drawings.

Photographs contained within the text carry the appropriate attributions. Mention has already been made of the contributions of both Peter Copland and the Imperial War Museum, in addition to which I must express my gratitude for their help and advice, to Mme Maryse Collet, of the Ecomusée de Saint-Nazaire, and M. Olivier Simoncelli, of the Etablissement de Communication et de Production Audiovisuelle de la Défense (ECPAD). Where it has been necessary to copy or enhance originals, I have relied heavily on the equipment and skills of Mr Ian McLeod, and Andy Lawrence (KUDIS: Keele University). For her willing, and continuing, assistance in translating numerous French texts I must make special mention of my niece, Mrs Sharon Greenwood.

As we now live in an age where digital forms of communication are becoming the norm, the text contains numerous references to Internet sites of value to tourists and researchers alike. Within this group two stand out as having been particularly useful – that of the Mairie; www.mairie-saintnazaire.fr and that of the highly informative www.franceguide.com.

On a final and very personal note, I have benefited greatly from the assistance, always given willingly, of Mme Michèle and M. Jacques Mahé, of Saint-Marc-sur-Mer. Their local knowledge and connections with those whose function it is to maintain accurate historical records of Saint-Nazaire and the surrounding area, have promoted a much deeper understanding, on my part, of the effects of the war in general, and the raid in particular, on the local French civilian population.

INDEX